FERAL MEDIA?

THE CHAMBERLAIN CASE, 40 YEARS ON

Dr Belinda Middleweek is a Senior Lecturer in Journalism at the University of Technology Sydney. She has a background in commercial television news production and factual entertainment, having worked on investigative crime documentaries for Graham McNeice Productions, Beyond International and iKandy Films. Her co-authored book *Real Sex Films: The New Intimacy and Risk in Cinema* (OUP, 2017) explored representations of intimacy, risk and transgression in an emerging cinematic movement. She has published on the subjects of media, celebrity, gender, deviance, human-robot interactions and digital activism in the journals *Feminist Media Studies*, *Journalism*, *Sexualities* and *Crime, Media, Culture*.

FERAL MEDIA?

THE CHAMBERLAIN CASE, 40 YEARS ON

BELINDA MIDDLEWEEK

Australian Scholarly

First published 2021 by
Australian Scholarly Publishing Ltd
7 Lt Lothian St Nth, North Melbourne, Vic 3051
Tel: 03 9329 6963 / Fax: 03 9329 5452
enquiry@scholarly.info / www.scholarly.info

ISBN 978-1-922454-45-4

Cover design: Amelia Walker

CONTENTS

ACKNOWLEDGEMENTS

This book is based on research for my PhD thesis and sincere thanks to Associate Professor Brigid Rooney at the University of Sydney for her guiding supervision. For her associate supervision, my thanks to Professor Catharine Lumby whose work and wordsmithery continue to inspire me.

Emeritus Professor Graham Seal AM and Professor Mark Deuze provided encouraging feedback and enriched the book with their insights and expertise. Thanks to Barry McKay for his careful proofread of the manuscript. Any errors are my own.

Thanks to my colleague Professor Phil Hayward at the University of Technology Sydney for a pre-seminar chat that gave me both the title 'Feral Media' and the courage to revisit my thesis all these years later. For being a generous mentor and friend, thanks to Professor Anne Cranny-Francis.

Heartfelt thanks to my mother Roslyn and Cosmo, for his endless cups of tea.

LIST OF ILLUSTRATIONS

Chapter 1

Chapter 2

Chapter 3

Chapter 4

Conclusion

INTRODUCTION

Lindy Chamberlain has an uncanny ability to incite emotional extremes. A cursory glance of the Twitter hashtags #thedingotookmybaby #dingobaby #LindyChamberlain #MichaelChamberlain #Azaria and #Australiantruecrime offers a breathtaking array of views about a woman who became a walking headline:

> The dingo took me baby lindy chaimblyn is aust biggest bogan ever!
>
> I always think of lindy's tube socks before I think of the dingo.
>
> Not everyone in Aust thought the Chamberlains were guilty, only the sheep who followed the media [sic].[1]

Forty years ago, the mother of Australia's 'dingo baby' was the most hated woman in Australia. The facts are well-known: in the absence of a body, a weapon or a motive, Lindy was convicted of the murder of her nine-and-a-half-week-old daughter, Azaria, who disappeared from a holiday campsite in the central Australian desert on 17 August 1980. She served three-and-a-half years in prison before the discovery of a crucial piece of exonerating evidence. When British tourist David James Brett fell to his death after climbing 'Ayers Rock' (now Uluru), police discovered a baby's matinee jacket next to his body – the same item of clothing Lindy maintained her daughter wore on the night of her disappearance. As a result, Lindy was released from prison on licence in 1986 and the convictions against the Chamberlains (her then husband, Michael, received a suspended sentence) were quashed two years later. However, the court's open finding on Azaria's disappearance continued to dog the Chamberlains, arousing further suspicion about their story of a dingo abduction. It was not until the fourth inquest in June 2012 that a coroner's verdict resolved doubt (legally at least) that a dingo had taken the sleeping infant from her tent as Lindy had maintained.

Long before the advent of social media platforms Facebook, Twitter and Instagram, Lindy was the topic of national conversation. At the time of her murder trial in 1982, 70 per cent of Australians believed her guilty of infanticide.[2] According to the prosecution, Lindy had slit her daughter's throat with a pair of nail scissors under the dashboard of the family's car and stuffed the infant's body inside a camera bag. In response, many used macabre humour to make sense of the tragedy with jokes such as 'Have you heard Olivia Newton-John's new song?' 'Hopelessly Devoured by You'. Others channelled their expressions in folkloric songs. 'Ode to Azaria' was sung to the tune of Australia's unofficial anthem 'Waltzing Matilda' and ended with the ghost of Azaria singing 'Mummy was the one who did away with me'.[3] Many Australians wrote to Lindy, often anonymously, using offensive language and inciting violence and mob justice: 'Lindy you should be hung up to the nearest tree', 'stuck up looking bitch … you ought to hang your head in shame' and 'your so bloody hard no tears have ever come out of your eyes … what a bad tempered bitch you are' [sic].[4] Others poured their apologies and support into letters of contrition ('Sorry I didn't make more of an effort to help you', one wrote) and followed Lindy's plight with 'heartfelt interest'.[5] Often, they described themselves as 'quiet, good living people and not cruel' who had apparently inoculated themselves from the 'media driven hysteria'.[6]

There are longstanding beliefs about the media's responsibility for the injustice Lindy and Michael endured. In the opera *Lindy* (2002), director Moya Henderson portrayed 'the media's' response to the Chamberlains in a 'howling chorus' of mongrel journalists, 'Ding', 'Dong', 'Belle' and 'Co', who writhed and sang their way across the stage in a sexually promiscuous display. In scholarly research on the Chamberlain case, there are plentiful references to the 'Australian dingo press'[7] and the 'baying journalistic dingoes and their publishers',[8] whose treatment of the Chamberlains, particularly Lindy, amounted to the 'fervid imagining of a sensationalising, unscrupulous and frequently misogynous media'.[9] So widely accepted is the trial by media thesis that educational institutions use the Chamberlain event as a case study in 'the nature of media circuses, public hype and trial by media – not only in Australia but internationally'.[10] The 40th anniversary of Azaria's disappearance is no different. Promoters of a speaking engagement to mark the event billed Lindy as 'the woman behind one of Australia's most tragic episodes of trial by media'.[11] For the injustice the Chamberlains suffered, Australian news media have shouldered the blame. Feral media. Indisputable. Fact.

I've spent more than 20 years investigating the media's role in the Chamberlain case, initially for a PhD thesis, and subsequently for research published in academic journal articles, a co-produced ABC Radio documentary,[12] in media interviews, in consultancy for a *New York Times* investigative documentary and now for this book. Over the course of my investigations, I interviewed Lindy and her former husband, the late Michael Chamberlain, along with journalists Malcolm Brown, Bill Hitchings and Shane Maguire; poured over hundreds of multimedia archives at the National Library of Australia (NLA) and the National Screen and Sound Archive (now Screensound); documented decades of newspaper and magazine circulation statistics at the Audit Bureau of Circulations; analysed reams of news print on microfilm across 26 local and international print publications; transcribed hours of news and current affairs television footage; and was the first to systematically examine a collection of Chamberlain activist pamphlets and newsletters at the State Library of New South Wales. The research took me across the Australian outback and from Cambridge University Library to our nation's capital where, in 2012, I presented at a ceremony hosted by the National Museum of Australia to commemorate the museum's purchase of the family's canary-yellow Holden Torana hatchback for their permanent collection. It was the same vehicle in which the family had travelled on their fateful holiday to the Rock and, thereafter, became a key piece of forensic evidence in the prosecution's case against the Chamberlains. Years later, somewhat mockingly, Michael changed the vehicle's number plate to 4ENSIC.

As my fellow band of 'Chamberlain-ologists' have demonstrated, there are many and varied perspectives on the legal, ethical, social and cultural impacts of the saga. I say 'band' because although we might be united in our examination of the wider implications of the case on Australian society, we don't always agree, and, like all good bands, we sometimes have our tiffs. So, on the role of the media in this saga, I tend to be a solo artist. There is little doubt the Chamberlains, and Lindy in particular, were the focus of a maelstrom of media publicity – chased by press photographers outside court; hounded by news cameras on a school fun run; secretly taped by police and journalists in an undercover sting and pursued by news helicopters that circled the family's home in Avondale College, Cooranbong. Whether it was her choice of dress, averted gaze or guilty 'look', the public often interpreted the Chamberlain case through media representations of its principal subject, Lindy, who – at turns – appeared as a 'little fairy', 'wicked witch' or 'lipstick vixen'. According to news reports, even the success of Lindy's defence case could be measured against her fleeting facial expression or the dress she wore to court each day. But the situation is far more complex. Let's take Lindy's comments about the media. Here is what she said in her autobiography *Through My Eyes*:

> Why blame the media? It is the public who demand the goods – so if there is no news today – well, spice it up to what the public wants or 'produce' some, and they do, and up go the reaction of demand and money and supply and greed. None can be blamed alone. All must share

– producer, reporter and consumer public.[13]

As a lightning rod for the nation's hostility, a headline-generator and the victim of a grave miscarriage of justice, Lindy Chamberlain was surprisingly candid in her comments about the burden of responsibility shared by the media and Australian public. So too was celebrated Australian author Frank Moorhouse in his questioning of the trial by media claims in a research article written in 1993 for the *Australian Cultural History* journal. In that article Moorhouse opposed the view that the media 'caused or sponsored the irrational lines of thinking' about the Chamberlains and urged the intellectual community to conduct a 'thorough analysis of the media coverage'.[14] It was a challenge I hefted in hand in my PhD thesis and now this book – to offer a critical analysis of news media coverage of the Chamberlain case.

But why a revisionist perspective you may ask? The legal case has already spanned four coronial inquests, a trial, two appeals and a Royal Commission of Inquiry. Hasn't the case clutched enough airtime and spilled enough ink? As this book seeks to demonstrate, viewing the case through the lens of history can offer powerful insights. With hindsight, academics, journalists, social commentators and critics, film producers, artists and dramatists have an opportunity to explore new interpretations of the event, especially as personal and public archives are discovered. One of those collections includes pamphlets written by Chamberlain activists, now housed at the State Library of New South Wales (see Chapter 2). There is also much to be analysed in a case whose limbs have stretched across four decades of Australian history. Though Azaria's disappearance at 'Ayers Rock' occurred on 17 August 1980, the legal proceedings only resolved in June 2012 when Coroner Elizabeth Morris concluded that a dingo had taken Azaria from her family's tent. At each milestone anniversary the case continues to pique public interest and is now an historical reference point for other instances of judicial miscarriage and dingo attacks on children. Indeed, at the time of writing, Lindy has become a media elder stateswoman – an obliging and often quoted expert source in news articles. Similarly, the moniker 'Lindy' is shorthand for any grave miscarriage of justice with much public debate about the 'Lindyfication' of controversial figures such as outback attack victim Joanne Lees, One Nation party founder Pauline Hanson and even Cardinal George Pell, Australia's highest ranking Catholic, who was convicted and later exonerated by Australia's High Court of charges of sexual offences against children.

Another reason to revisit the media's role in this saga is because the Chamberlain case is inseparable from the media representations it generated and, as such, is Australia's first modern media event. Early on, we judged Lindy's demeanour from her media appearances. Who could forget the unfortunate television interview in which Lindy detailed how the dingo would have taken Azaria? She told the reporter that, 'They [dingoes] use their feet like hands and pull back the skin as they go and they just peel it like an orange';[15] or the photographs of Lindy attending the Supreme Court trial in her billowing frocks, a 'new maternity dress each day' for the heavily pregnant accused.[16] Arguably, media coverage of the case was unparalleled in Australia. I say 'arguably' because other spectacular events have commanded bold headlines, such as the capture of bush outlaw Ned Kelly in 1880, the moon landing in 1969 and the disappearance of Kings Cross publisher Juanita Nielson in 1975. But Azaria's disappearance was the first 'modern' media event following advancements in communication, cable and satellite technologies in the 1980s that gave spectacle to live audiences, as proceeding chapters will make clear.

In this book I deploy the term 'media event' in its common domain usage as a media-driven phenomenon that is complex, spectacular and dynamically unfolding in time. For Daniel Dayan and Elihu Katz, media events are 'interruptions of routine that intervene in the normal flow of broadcasting and our lives'.[17] They record significant moments in history, rather than routine news stories such as sporting match results, stock market fluctuations or government policy announcements. The

Chamberlain case comprised a series of 'exceptional moments' that can be understood 'in the sense of singular irruptions into the regular flow of media experience'.[18] The most spectacular among them were Coroner Denis Barritt's decision to live-telecast his findings at the first inquest in February 1981 (see Chapter 1); Channel Nine's exclusive interview with Lindy following her shock release from prison in 1986 (see Chapter 3); and Coroner Elizabeth Morris' invitation to ABC News Darwin to deliver her findings on Azaria's disappearance, direct to the nation, at the fourth and final coronial inquest in June 2012 (see Conclusion). These moments prefigured the central role of television in our lives, particularly in the latter half of the 20th century. By commanding the eyeballs of local and international audiences, they soldered people together on a mass scale and were instrumental in processes of nation-building at the time. Despite the waning influence of television in a post-broadcast era dominated by social media behemoths, digital media technologies and dispersed audiences, media events continue to survive in innovative formats and evidence the increasing mediatisation of our lives.[19]

In considering the Chamberlain case as a 'media event', this book is divided into four chapters that track reportage of the case across time and situate the saga in contemporary media debates about trolling, selfies, Insta-celebrity, and hashtag activism. From the perspective of 21st-century digital media, this book will ask important questions about an event that has been reported, debated and dissected for four decades such as, how was Azaria's disappearance represented in the Australian media? How have those media representations shifted across time? How do traditional media and social media responses to the Chamberlain case compare? This latter question enables us to consider whether the kinds of anti-social behaviours we see whelped in online communication platforms were rehearsed four decades earlier in public responses to the Chamberlain case.

Chapter 1 begins when news first broke of a dingo abduction in the shadow of Australia's iconic 'Ayers Rock'.[20] At this time, the circumstances of the event – a baby's disappearance in the outback – framed media reports about the incident. But within six weeks, the news story was eclipsed by the case's central characters – Azaria, the dingo, the parents, religion and the landscape – in what was shorthand for the event itself. The emphasis on characters or 'personalities' rather than the reported facts of the story represents a shift towards entertainment-based news that is now a hallmark of contemporary journalism. Whether in reports about the rise of teen sexting, 'thinspo' posts on social media or the sex-robot revolution, our daily news digest is now filled with the personalities, private lives and private parts (!) of regular people. But this wasn't always the case. Indeed, developments in the reportage of the Chamberlain case signalled wider changes in news media production and delivery that were transforming the industry in the 1980s, thus laying the groundwork for 21st century journalism in Australia.

It is very easy to attribute trolling to digital communications technology where anti-social behaviours are ubiquitous. Who hasn't received a hate-filled missive from an invisible foe lurking in the corners of their social media channels? As I argue in Chapter 2, trolling and other irreverent, playful and ardent speech acts were rehearsed by hundreds of self-described 'ordinary' Australians in the range of notes they wrote, mainly to Lindy, to express their opinions about the dingo baby case. Now housed in the National Library of Australia and filed in the Chamberlain Papers under the headings 'nut', 'nasty' and 'unusual',[21] the more unsavoury expressions resemble the antagonisms we see on social media today. Other letters in the collection are heartfelt and sympathetic, and their views chimed with the Chamberlain activists whose coordinated newsletters and pamphlets comprised a formidable counter-public in opposition to the guilty verdict, and which are now held in a separate collection at the State Library of New South Wales. Together, these writings represent one of the greatest demonstrations of public opinion expression in Australia. Chapter 2 draws parallels between modern-day behaviours on social media, and public utterances about the Chamberlain case that were channelled in mainstream and alternate media.

Every day on social media we delve into the lives of would-be celebrities. On Instagram, users with sizeable followings and demonstrated cultural influence parade their ever-changing wardrobes, inspirational hashtags and perfected *moues.* Using selfies and other self-presentational media,[22] these 'influencers' promote highly curated lifestyles and products such as vegan diet shakes, açaí bowls and date-filled protein balls. As I argue in Chapter 3, the lives and loves of ordinary people weren't always so titillating. Historically, celebrity was a condition or attribute endowed by noble birth, recognised in individual skill and achievement or a signal of a person's value and worth. However, by the late 20th century, changes in the context of celebrity production provided the conditions necessary for a bobby-socked pastor's wife to become a household name. In Chapter 3, I trace fundamental changes to the celebrity system that facilitated Lindy's promulgation from ordinary woman to 'face of the 80s' in Australia.[23]

'Ayers Rock' has always loomed large in the Chamberlain story. It was in the Rock's shadow that a dingo snatched Azaria from her tent, and nearly six years later that the stout monument would release from its craggy clutches the infant's matinee jacket after a climber fell to his death. News coverage of these key moments in the Chamberlain story coincided with landmark events in the nation's social and cultural history, including the passing of Aboriginal Land Rights (NSW) legislation in 1983; the symbolic 'Ayers Rock' handover ceremony in 1985; and the 1988 bicentennial commemorations of the arrival of the First Fleet of British convict ships into Sydney Harbour, which marked the beginning of Australia's European colonial history. Broader conversations about Australian national identity and the dispossession of Australia's First People were channelled in media coverage of the Chamberlain case that provided a vehicle for discussions about nationhood, race and identity in the 1980s. Chapter 4 traces debates in media about the meaning of these national events, often read through the Chamberlain case reportage, that continue today in #BLM protests and a cultural ambivalence towards Indigenous activism best summed up in the slogan 'sorry (not sorry)'.

In all, this book argues that media representations enhance our understanding of the infant's disappearance and, more broadly, our own development as a nation on the cusp of the 21st century. For 40 years the Australian news media have been, and remain, the focus of ire, reproach and condemnation for the persecution of the Chamberlains. On this, the anniversary of Azaria's disappearance, let's reconsider the evidence and weigh claims of a 'feral media'.

CHAPTER 1

MEDIA BEFORE MEGXIT

> … with all its characters and identities, the [Azaria] case has tended to creak a little at the joints.[1]

In February 2020, on the Facebook page of Australia's popular current affairs program *60 Minutes*, producers uploaded a teaser video in promotion of an upcoming story about Megxit. A month earlier *The Sun* had coined the catchphrase Megxit in an all-caps headline following the shock announcement that the Duke and Duchess of Sussex would be leaving their senior royal stations and taking a 'revised media approach'. UK media outlets took brutal aim at the headlining royal couple whose actions reportedly showed their selfishness and the increasing irrelevance of the monarchy.[2] Alongside the Megxit promo, *60 Minutes* posted a dusty 1986 episode of Ray Martin's exclusive interview with Lindy and her then husband Michael. The throwback interview with the Chamberlains was likely to capitalise on the 40th anniversary of Azaria's disappearance later that year. Viewer reactions ran the gamut of emotions:

> Oh poor Lindy … NOT!!
>
> You go camping … you take care of your babies!!! From Dogs and humans!!! [sic]
>
> I guess we will never know the truth but one thing. I didn't see any tears when she cried. Curious.
>
> Great actress.
>
> Guilty as sin.
>
> This was typically trial by media aided by the opinions of Bored Housewives. Trump is 100% correct when he calls the media the enemy of the people.
>
> If your reading this Lindy I would love to apologise. I was only young when we watched you on 60 minutes. I made a choice to believe you were guilty. Years after, I became a mother and after that my opinion changed. I'm sorry I didn't believe you, I'm truly sorry for everything you hade to endure [sic].

These impassioned responses are typical of the way Lindy Chamberlain continues to polarise Australian public opinion. Like Markle, she exists in a socio-political context that imposes 'ever higher costs for "visible" women'.[3] This is no more apparent than in the ways we understand the ramifications of that visibility, whether it's in the 'Lindyfication' of Australians wrongfully persecuted or the coining of #Megxit, a hashtag inspired by Britain's Brexit deal and deeply 'rooted in a social media campaign of hate' against the Duchess.[4] Even in the snapshot of online posts about Lindy, the socio-political context of Brexit, with its importation of Trump's 'post-truth politics', is clearly evident.[5] As one poster declared as the reason for Lindy's persecution: 'Trump is 100% correct when he calls the media the enemy of the people'. Though the conditions of their visibility differed, Lindy and Meghan are historical reference points on a continuum of representations of public-facing women in the western world. Their media portrayals reveal the complicated interactions between high-profile women and news outlets, as Chapter 3 will explore. Where the stories of Lindy and Meghan collide on the Facebook page of *60 Minutes*, we see a surprising degree of engagement with a 40-year-old news story that predated the digital revolution and the likes of Facebook, Instagram and Twitter. At last count, there were 538 emojis and 400 viewer comments about the throwback Chamberlain interview on *60 Minutes*. That was double the number of reactions to the Megxit teaser. But when Azaria disappeared in August 1980, newspapers were still king.

The nation's printing plates were well inked in the months before Azaria's disappearance. Merchant banker, lawyer and co-founder of the Nugan Hand Bank, Francis John Nugan, was found dead in mysterious circumstances in January of that year: Australia's first 'test tube baby', Candice Reed, was born in Melbourne's Royal Women's Hospital and, to much acclaim, Queen Elizabeth II and Prince Philip opened the new High Court of Australia building on their royal tour in May. As Azaria Chamberlain's disappearance occurred on a Sunday, commonly regarded in the industry as a slow news day, the majority of reports were delayed 24 hours. The isolated location of 'Ayers Rock' further hampered efforts to confirm details of the attack. It was not until Tuesday 19 August (nearly two days later), that the majority of Australia's newspapers reported the incident. Two Sydney dailies were the exception: *The Sun* and its rival the *Daily Mirror* together broke the news of a dingo attack in the outback in their afternoon editions on Monday 18 August 1980 (Figures 1.1 and 1.2). Both newspapers headlined the infant's disappearance, employing a similar strategy in the use of the word 'snatch' to convey the infant's sudden seizure, with 'Baby girl snatched by dingo'[6] and 'Dingoes snatch baby girl'.[7] On the following day *The Australian* reported Azaria's disappearance in a similar fashion with the headline 'Killer dingo snatches baby'.[8] A 'killer dingo' was also the culprit in the Brisbane *Courier-Mail*'s story coverage headlined 'No Trace of Killer Dingo'.[9] Across Sydney and Brisbane newspapers as well as the national broadsheet, the attack was reported to be swift and brutal.

However, within six weeks of Azaria's disappearance a distinct change occurred in media reports of the tragedy. Around October 1980, focus on the event – a dingo attack on a baby in central Australia – shifted to the story's leading characters: the dingo, the mother Lindy, the victim, 'Ayers Rock' and the family's Adventist religion. But for journalist Bill Hitchings, who covered the story extensively for the Melbourne *Herald*, news workers didn't have to dramatise the story, it was ready-made:

> … it was the handsome young couple, the baby, Ayers Rock, the dingo, the black trackers, the whole bit, and religion, all those things brought it together and it was just tailor made … people say that the media sensationalised it, they didn't have to, it was a sensational news report.[10]

Rather than mere textual descriptions, fleeting figures or incidental news items, these characters became highly identifiable and durable metaphors in news coverage of the story. Personalisation is often regarded as a 'tabloid news factor'[11] associated with a popular market-style of reporting that's been historically maligned for its sensationalism and 'sexualised news agenda'.[12] We need only recall the British *Sun* newspaper's introduction in the 1970s of the scantily clad 'Page 3 Girl' that earned print baron Rupert Murdoch the dubious title of purveyor of 'bonk journalism'. Nowadays, a liberated nipple is a social media-driven political statement (think: #freethenipple) rather than a titillating titbit that a style of gent might enjoy before wrapping up his fish and chips. In our always switched-on digital news environment, we're accustomed to reading news stories about, say, the rise in sexting among teens, the mental health impacts of 'pro-ana' (favouring anorexic) Snapchat communities, the worrying trend of 'thinspo' (thin inspiration) posts on TikTok or the men who swap their girlfriends for sex robots (no more 'not tonight dear, I have a headache'). Our daily news digest is filled with the personalities, private lives and private parts of regular people. But this wasn't always the case; news wasn't always so intimate and personal.

The popularity of tabloids in the 1980s was interpreted as a sign of the decline in traditional standards of news-making and even the moral decay in society.[13] This was in part due to the perception that tabloids delivered snack news – colourfully packaged content that failed to satiate or offer readers a well-balanced news diet. We can trace that perception to the origins of the term. 'Tabloid', a portmanteau of the words 'tablet' and 'alkaloid', was originally a trademark for concentrated drugs and medicines in tablet form registered by the British pharmaceutical company Burroughs, Wellcome & Company. The firm's co-founder, Henry Wellcome, the American entrepreneur after whom the Wellcome Collection in central London was later named, coined the term 'tabloid' when he awoke at 4.30 am one morning in 1884 with a stroke of genius.[14] He dispatched his secretary at that early hour to dictate a memo and the tabloid was born.[15] Other products in Burroughs, Wellcome and Co's pharmaceutical range of 'tabloids' included compressed tea and a range of tonics and laxatives with intestinal clearing labels such as 'Tabloid Livingstone Rouser' and 'Tabloid Forced March'.[16] With such origins, it's little surprise print tabloids might be associated with more vulgar news appetites.

In the pre-digital era, the tabloid referred to a condensed version of news that was half the size of a traditional 'broadsheet' newspaper. But it was more than just size that counted. The tabloid became known for its popular presentation, accessibility and style of news that lacked the 'objectivity' of 'quality' counterparts in the broadsheet press.[17] Its chief characteristics included informal and sometimes sensationalised language, bold typeface, personalised narratives and characters, the increased use of visual images, appeals to humour, audience incentives and niche tailoring to meet market imperatives.[18] What Elizabeth Bird calls 'true tabloids' can be traced to Britain in the first decade of the 20th century and to the following decade in the US with the likes of William Randolph Hearst's *Daily Mirror* that was launched in New York City in 1924.[19] Others have traced the phenomenon to an earlier period in Australia with characteristics often decried as tabloid found in *The Sydney Gazette* (1803), *The Referee* (1886–1939) and *The Arrow* (1889–1933) newspapers.[20] It was not until the 1980s that the term 'tabloidisation' was first used in America to bemoan the increased adoption of tabloid characteristics in 'quality' news media, either in print or television.[21] With the shift to digital in the late 1990s, tabloidese reporting found a new home online. At the forefront of this trend was the entertainment news site and television channel TMZ (or 'thirty mile zone' in reference to the 'studio zone' in Los Angeles), which was founded in 2005.[22]

Chiefly visible in the 1980s then, was an intensification of so-called tabloid practices – examined here in the shift to character-driven reportage. The position taken throughout this book is that continued public debate about the declining standards of news, as evident in the popular appeal of tabloids, is often based on elitist, outdated and moralising assumptions about what journalism should or ought to be. As media scholar

Catharine Lumby explains, these views emanate from the rarefied realms of those 'in the know' and other experts who determine which issues are important and their legitimate treatment in news media.[23] By contrast, it's in the arena of tabloids, including talkback radio programs, downscale commercial current affairs television programs and women's magazines, that we most often hear from ordinary people.[24] Historically, the domain of the tabloids has been a far more inclusive, democratic and diverse space than traditional quality media would allow.[25] This is not to overlook the ethical concerns tabloid practices raise, but to suggest that we can better understand media reportage of the Chamberlain case by situating it within broader structural shifts taking place in the Australian media industry; shifts precipitated by increased market competition and the rapid development of communications technology. But firstly, who were those characters carved in early news reports of Azaria's disappearance?

The Dingo

Weighing 10 to 15 kilograms, the dingo is Australia's largest land predator with a pedigree spanning 4,000 years.[26] The animal was highly valued in traditional Indigenous communities as companion, protector and hunting dog. Ancestral dingoes played an important role in Dreaming stories, figuring in songs and ceremonies.[27] Recent research has found Aboriginal women fostered a particularly close bond with dingoes: the women carried their pups around their waists like babies, rubbed the dingoes in ochre to ward off evil spirits, and accorded the animals special burial status when they died.[28] In early 20th century settler narratives, the dingo's haunting howl and predatory behaviour towards livestock contributed to its reputation as a marauder. Historically, the dingo has shapeshifted from wily beast and cunning thief to sometime larrikin.[29] In particular, print media coverage of the Azaria dingo revived the animal's cultural status as petty thief in reports about its stealthy behaviour. Wollongong's *Illawarra Mercury* reported 'A shape just like a dingo … slinking out of the tent',[30] while Orange's *Central Western Daily* described a covert dingo that made 'no sound' when it carried Azaria off in its mouth.[31] For the *Daily Mirror*, 'a pack of dingoes' 'snatched' Azaria in their 'jaws',[32] while *The Age* reported the 'dingo [was] on the run from man'.[33] For Chamberlain scholar Noel Sanders, the tendency of newspapers to portray the dingo as a thief is a legacy of early convict narratives:

> The dingo stands as a metaphor for thieves, criminals and the poor in Australia, as a metaphor for aggressors against property, in fact, rather than as murderer.[34]

Some have even argued Lindy's description of Azaria's disappearance tapped into these fervid cultural imaginings. On the family's sombre return home from 'their camping trip', Lindy stopped at the 'Ayers Rock' store and inscribed a message in the visitor's book. Intending to warn people about the dingo menace in the local area, she wrote simply, 'A dingo took my baby'. Her use of the word 'took' is an illustration of popular beliefs about the dingo's thieving behaviour rather than a description of its murderous actions.[35] Not only was the dingo anthropomorphised in early reports of Azaria's disappearance but also clothed in sympathy. He was an outsider, among the downtrodden, and an underdog in Anglo-Australian cultural mythology. It was no surprise then that at the Chamberlains' trial for murder, protestors outside the court wore the 'Dingo is Innocent' t-shirts, believing the animal had been scapegoated.

The Mother

A native of New Zealand's Whakatane in the North Island, Lindy's family moved to Victoria where her father was appointed a pastor in the Seventh-day Adventist Church. In 1969 she married an Adventist pastor, the New Zealand born Michael Chamberlain. Lindy had been schooled in religious stoicism and was not prone to dramatic display. So, it was somewhat of an irony – given accusations of her cold and emotionless demeanour at the murder trial years later – that early media reports described Lindy's 'frantic' emotional state and inner torment after finding baby Azaria missing from the family tent. *The Daily Telegraph*'s first report of the incident captured her agony in the headline, 'Anguished mum tells: I saw my baby stolen by dingo'.[36] Frequent references to 'the baby's mother', 'the woman' or the 'wife of Pastor Michael Chamberlain',[37] rather than the use of Lindy's full name, suggest the narrow, gender-inflected and socially circumscribed roles she occupied in the initial media coverage. It was not until the Supreme Court trial in 1982 that reports about 'Azaria's mother'[38] were replaced with the moniker 'Lindy'. As John Bryson – the author of the bestselling book on the case, *Evil Angels* – so accurately observed, by the time the Supreme Court trial started 'No one now referred to her any other way, even in newspaper headlines. "Lindy" was a name now more familiar to the nation than the first names of footballers and tennis stars.'[39] It was also from Lindy's perspective that we began to learn of the infant's fate in headlines such as 'Anguished mum tells: I saw my baby stolen by dingo'.[40] The reporting of events from a personalised viewpoint enables easy reader identification with the news subject and is characteristic of a tabloid news style.[41] Chapter 3 will probe further Lindy's 'celebrification' in the context of her transformation from unknown pastor's wife to household name.

The Victim

Early news coverage of Azaria's disappearance emphasised the infant's tender age with variations of 'missing baby',[42] the 'baby hunt',[43] the 'baby search'[44] and the 'baby girl'[45] used interchangeably in a range of reports. As *The Sun* described, she was just a 'baby girl' from Mt Isa 'weigh[ing] ten pounds' and on holidays with her family before her disappearance.[46] By October 1980, however, news reports became increasingly provocative. Drawing on the conventions of crime reportage, the police investigation into Azaria's disappearance was described as a 'hunt' and the case itself a 'mystery' and a 'riddle' that could only be solved with 'clues'.[47] So too did references to Azaria's nubile innocence transform in news reports implying a secret physical deformity. *The Sun* reported rumours she was a 'spastic' child and 'sickly baby', sacrificed by her parents in a religious cleansing ritual.[48] As the years unfolded, the name 'Azaria' or 'Dingo baby'[49] – a sobriquet that would often be confused with a juvenile dingo – would become as familiar to us as an iconic brand on the supermarket shelf.

'The Rock'

Taller than the Eiffel Tower in Paris or the Chrysler Building in New York, 'Ayers Rock' rises 348 metres above the surrounding landscape. Much was made of the fact Azaria disappeared in the grounds of the 600-million-year-old red welt, a remote location known as 'the red centre', 'the dead centre' and the 'holy navel' of Australia.[50] In initial news reports of the dingo abduction, many focused on the remote locality and size of 'the Rock', with one regional newspaper in New South Wales, declaring the crime scene to be 'out there',[51] while *The Courier-Mail* mockingly 'narrowed' the location of 'the famous Rock' to just '1000km from Adelaide'.[52] International newspapers insinuated 'the Rock' contributed to Azaria's disappearance, with the London *Observer* newspaper reporting the location as: 'an eerie and unsettling place which seemed as if the thing itself had played a part in the events'.[53] In a slew of local and international newspapers the 'thing' was beginning to resemble, if not a perpetrator, then a silent, complicit witness to Azaria's disappearance. Reports of Azaria vanishing in 'dingo country' amidst 'terrain [which] was too bad' and beset by 'freezing temperatures' imparted a sense of foreboding and doom.[54]

Depictions of the Northern Territory landscape as an inhospitable, mysterious locale characterised much of the Chamberlain news coverage. Reporting on the Supreme Court trial in Darwin, Malcolm Brown described the 'Top End' as 'the most natural place of all for the Azaria saga to come' since it revealed the 'jarring oddities' of a people characterised by the harshness of their landscape.[55] Brown's 'outsider' perspective enabled him to situate Azaria's disappearance in a remote landscape that time and progress had yet to 'civilise'.

> Subtler manifestations of the isolation [of Alice Springs] take longer to materialise: stories from the friendly local people about the hazards of falling ill, of obtaining a new windscreen, the price of some fresh produce ($2.50 for a kilo of pears), the late arrival of the daily interstate newspapers ('The Age' costs $1).[56]

The rough, slow and isolated country from which Azaria disappeared was often contrasted with the urban sophistication of city locales where many journalists typed their copy. It showed a tendency among newsmakers to use the setting of the dingo attack as a framing device for the story and, indeed, highlighted class and racial divides between 'settled' Australia and its unruly, barren centre (see Chapter 4).

The Religion

At the time of Azaria's disappearance, Michael Chamberlain was a minister in the little-known spiritual community of Seventh-day Adventism on the fringe of mainstream Protestant Christian ideology. Adventists, as they are known, observe a Saturday sabbath and follow Old Testament dietary requirements. Abstinence is akin to godliness and many strict adherents avoid smoking, consuming alcohol, caffeinated drinks, hot condiments and spices, and follow a vegetarian diet. The Sanitarium Health Food Company, which started with a small bakery in Northcote, Melbourne, in 1898, was likely the only exposure Australians had to Seventh-day Adventism. Yet within two years, it was enough to headline a story 'My sister Lindy: God still loves her'[57] for readers to know exactly the religion and the subject being reported.

In early news reports of the disappearance, the Chamberlains' religion was evident in source titling conventions. Lindy was described as 'a minister's wife' and Michael as a pastor in the Seventh-day Adventist Church.[58] But rumours about the origins of the name Azaria and the little known religious doctrine of Adventists soon surfaced in the press. It was enough for Lindy to address them directly in media interviews confirming that 'Azaria' did not mean 'sacrifice in the wilderness' and that any suggestion Azaria was a 'human sacrifice for our church is still very, very far-fetched'.[59] According to *The Sun-Herald*, the rising tide of secularism in Australia seemed to contribute to the public's growing scepticism about a dingo abduction as early as the first inquest in February 1981.

Today, when signs of Christian faith are perhaps

> not as abundant as they were, parents who had lost a baby might be excused for thinking harshly of their God, or writing him off altogether. The Chamberlains knelt and thanked their God. To them, Azaria's death simply showed He worked in mysterious ways.[60]

The Chamberlains' behaviour, particularly on the night of Azaria's disappearance, left many Australians confounded. Michael's eagerness to cooperate with the media by taking photographs of the campgrounds where his daughter went missing, the couple's decision to turn to prayer rather than join the initial search party and Lindy's dispassionate, stoic reaction to events, were interpreted by some as callous and evidence of their connection to a religious cult.[61] Malcolm Brown summed up mainstream opinion when he reported, 'It would be fair to call them an unusual people, if only because of their exceptional faith'.[62] Twelve months later, when the Supreme Court convicted Lindy for murder and Michael as an accessory after the fact, some newspapers cited Lindy's disruptive childhood as an explanation for Azaria's murder. In an exclusive report, *The Daily Telegraph* revealed Lindy's 'secret' and 'gypsy-like' lifestyle within the Adventist Church, declaring 'This – and other details of Lindy's life and background – [have] been one of the best kept secrets of the Dingo Baby saga'.[63] Her formative years were described as spent among the 'guardians of the secrets' or prelates of the Seventh-day Adventist Church.[64] It was even remarked by one print publication that '[Lindy's] parents did not even record her birth in the local paper, *The Beacon*' in Whakatane, New Zealand.[65] Indeed, the 'secret' rituals and unconventional practices of the Adventist Church informed media reportage of the case.

The altered tone of news reports just six weeks after Azaria's disappearance captured a rising cynicism in what the press dubbed 'the dingo theory'. In part this was achieved by pulling focus on the story's central characters to the extent that by 1982, as *The Sun-Herald* would opine, it was difficult to imagine a 'post-Azaria world – without the mystery, the Rock, the church, the dingoes'.[66] So well-worn were these characters that they began to 'creak a little at the joints'.[67] Aside from giving us a glimpse into tonal changes in news reports, characters forged out of the Azaria reportage made the story more accessible to a general readership, epitomised the complex issues the case soon raised about motherhood, national identity, belonging and religion, and were an attempt to make sense of unfathomable circumstances.

Transformations in news storytelling connected the Chamberlain case to wider structural changes occurring in the Australian media industry in the 1980s, which informed our understanding of the event and its public reception.

OVER ONE MILLION READERS

THE Sun

MONDAY, August 18, 1980

20 cents

CITY FINAL

SUPER VALUE

TRAGIC TOURIST COUPLE

BABY GIRL SNATCHED BY DINGO

CAMP RAID: 200 IN HUNT

A WILD animal — believed to be a dingo — snatched a baby girl from a tourist campsite at Ayers Rock last night and made off into the bush.

The baby's frantic mother, a minister's wife, believes she saw the wild dog flee with her infant in its mouth.

Bloodstains were found on the baby's sleeping bag.

More than 200 police, rangers and tourists today launched a massive search of scrubland around the campsite.

Searchers are scouring dingo lairs around Ayers Rock, but say they have little hope of finding the baby alive.

The baby's father, Seventh Day Adventist minister Pastor Michael Chamberlain, 36, said today he had given up hope of finding his daughter.

CONT P 2

OLIVIA STEPS OUT IN STYLE

By KERRY YATES

OLIVIA Newton-John is in Sydney with a new hairstyle.

She's had her long blonde locks layered into a shorter, softer style and feathered to frame her famous face.

The casual wash'n'wear hairstyle (you simply run your fingers through the hairstyle to comb it) will no doubt be copied by Olivia's fans.

It's easy. It works best on hair that is naturally

Continued Page 3

HOLIDAY STARS

THE SORT OF PEOPLE YOU GET ALONG WITH BEST

PAGES TODAY | WEATHER: Sunny periods. (Map P.37.) | LOTTERIES: Opera House 701, P.48; New Jackpot 1764, P.58. | FINANCE: P.44. | TV: P.22.

Figure 1.1

The Sun newspaper's headline coverage of the dingo attack on Azaria Chamberlain in the afternoon edition, 18 August 1980, *The Sun*, p. 1 [Fairfax]

LATE FINAL EXTRA

Daily Mirror

OVER 1 MILLION READERS

Monday, August 18, 1980 BIGGEST WEEK-DAY SALES IN NSW

THE 80s PAPER

20c

• No. 11,849 • PHONE: 2 0924 • LOTTERIES: Opera House 701, P35; Jackpot 1766, P36 • TV: P20 • FINANCE: P38 • WEATHER: Showers

DINGOES SNATCH BABY GIRL

Hundreds of people are searching near Ayers Rock for a 9-week-old girl believed to have been snatched from a tent by a pack of dingoes.

The baby's mother saw a dingo leaving the tent with something in its jaws but did not suspect it might be her child.

Police and trackers found dog paw marks near the tent.

• FULL STORY PAGE 2

ENVOY OLIVIA

Olivia Newton-John likes the idea of being an unofficial ambassador for Australia, the star of the film Xanadu told a press conference in Sydney today. Full story Page 8.

LAURIE OAKES REPORTS

BUDGET AID ON HOMES, FAMILY, PENSION

A better deal for first home buyers, families, pensioners and the unemployed is on the way in tomorrow's Federal Budget.

The full Home Savings Grant will go up to $43,000, phasing out at $33,000.

Families will benefit from a range of social welfare concessions.

DOLE MAY GO UP TOO

Single pensioners will get more than $3 a week extra and the combined married rate will increase by more than $5.

Full story Page 3

THY NEIGHBOUR'S WIFE

STARTS TODAY

Figure 1.2

The Daily Mirror newspaper's headline coverage of the dingo attack on Azaria Chamberlain in the afternoon edition, 18 August 1980, *The Daily Mirror*, p. 1 [News Limited]

Increased media competition and the growth of alternate communications technologies were among the developments. The box set revolution that began in Australia in 1956 with the introduction of television (and then colour transmission in 1975) fundamentally changed the way we consumed information including news content. In living rooms across the country and elsewhere, families were huddled around domestic televisions and soon setting their daily schedules to popular television programs *I Love Lucy* and *The Beverly Hillbillies*. The technology even changed mealtimes with frozen TV dinners that imitated the traditional family roast being sold in supermarket freezers. For Australian historian Keith Windschuttle, there were other changes impacting the Australian media landscape once dominated by print news outlets. With the onslaught of television, radio stations pivoted from night-time to day-time scheduling and were filled with news and current affairs content.[68] There were also changes to commuter travel where suburban sprawl led many to rely on private motor cars, rather than public transport, to get to and from work resulting in fewer newspaper sales for the journey.[69] Combined, these developments would fundamentally impact the way Australians consumed the news.

Television would also change the way audiences interacted with news that was suddenly intimate, up-close and unfolding in real time. In media coverage of the Chamberlain case, this was never more apparent than on Friday 20 February 1981 when, at 11.00 am, at least two million Australians tuned into an Alice Springs courtroom to watch Coroner Denis Barritt deliver his findings in the first coronial inquest into Azaria's disappearance. It was the first time in history that cameras had been permitted inside an Australian courtroom, thereby producing the nation's 'biggest courtroom gallery'.[70] As for ratings, the audience was around the same number as those transfixed to black and white television screens to witness the historic moon landing in July 1969.[71] In the weeks before the verdict, Channel Seven's head technician, Gary Tait, approached the Coroner to ask for principal rights to the live broadcast. It was granted on the condition that the network stream the findings to other commercial stations in a slightly delayed time format.[72]

There were concerns in the legal fraternity that televising a verdict may dramatize the court and those who appeared before it. Complicating matters was that recent interviews with politicians on commercial radio had shown them to be 'too often deflected from the real issues by posturing for their constituents whom they imagined to be listening'.[73] The televised promotion of Australian cricket had drawn similar concerns about the 'exaggeration of [the game's] grossest aspects at the expense of its subtle essence'.[74] Barritt anticipated fears about the dramatizing potential of the medium and ordered that the television camera be focused on his face alone. He was driven by a belief that audiences would be less likely to draw inferences if they were prevented from seeing the Chamberlains' reaction to the verdict. History would later find he miscalculated, with the publicity only intensifying the media gaze.

Debates in Australia about the televising of court verdicts were contemporaneous with those occurring internationally. In the United States in January 1981, Florida's Supreme Court decided that the civil rights of a defendant on trial for murder were not violated by the televising of a court's verdict, thereby enshrining the principle of trial by one's peers.[75] Even today, fears the broadcast of courtroom proceedings will degenerate into 'spectator sport' have received media coverage following the decision to televise high profile criminal cases in England and Wales.[76]

Some media scholars have found the televising of live court verdicts situates audiences in the moment. In his important work on the social history of broadcasting, Paddy Scannell describes this as a form of 'presencing':

> The 'liveness' of broadcast coverage is the key to its impact, since it offers the real sense of access to an event in its moment-by-moment unfolding. This 'presencing', this re-presenting of a present occasion to an absent audience, can powerfully produce the effect of being-there, of being

> involved (caught up) in the here-and-now of the occasion. This being in the moment, especially in its 'unfolding', creates the mood of expectancy: what's happening? what's next?[77]

So too, the Chamberlain broadcast 'captured a sense of the miraculous', which audiences associate with the enthralling power of television that is central to the construction of a media event.[78] Relayed intimately, up close and in real time, audiences could play a symbolic role in the dispensing of justice. An editorial in *The Sydney Morning Herald* the day after the historic broadcast applauded Barritt's decision to ensure transparency in the rule of law:

> As in the Azaria Chamberlain case, the television cameras rove and record events relating to court proceedings outside the courtrooms, and make their impressions on the public independently of what happens inside them. If the courts persist in holding aloof from this fact, they risk putting themselves increasingly out of the mainstream of public influence and credibility. Their adherence to protocol which does not recognise the invention of radio and television as added techniques for communication between

> the court and the public is less than quaint. The proposition that admitting television into the courtroom would encourage posturing by judges or counsel will cut no ice with those familiar with court proceedings. It could be argued with more conviction that the exposure of posturing to the public would do a lot to help stamp it out by arousing strong public disapproval.[79]

The Sydney Morning Herald 's editorial is to be expected given the news media's vested interest in the televising of court verdicts as a publicity opportunity, but not all journalists were persuaded by such arguments. For Malcolm Brown, the case's principal concern with death made the irony of a live verdict seem inappropriate, as he reported 'Australians crowded around TV sets in homes, offices and shop windows to watch a live judgment about death'.[80] For author John Bryson, the disturbing part about the two inquests was their focus on the Chamberlains rather than the deceased: 'Some Inquests are about the living, rather than the dead. Both Chamberlain inquests fell into that category'.[81] Ultimately, Barritt's finding that a dingo was responsible for Azaria's death and that her clothing had been interfered with by 'a person or persons unknown' was delivered to engrossed and highly mediated audiences. Mediated, that is, because the audience members bore a symbolic connection to one another via media despite differences in the hue of the crowd (age, gender, ethnicity) and the physical distances separating them. Such televisual exposure was a foretaste of things to come in media reporting of this landmark case.

The popularity of television content was not lost on print media proprietors who began placing greater emphasis on entertaining news formats with proven market appeal. As Rupert Murdoch foretold in his 1977 address to the Annual Convention of the American Newspaper Publishers Association, to survive, newspapers must broaden their readership by appealing to the 'everyday consumer'.[82] Figures from the Audit Bureau of Circulations – part of the bureaux providing the media industry with statistics on the number of newspapers sold – offered a pressing commercial reason to nab the attentions of the popular market. In most Australian states in the late 1970s and early 1980s, newspaper sales were dwindling. Net paid circulation figures (or newspapers sold) up to 31 March 1980 were in decline, with the only notable exceptions being *The Australian*, *The Age*, and *The Northern Territory News*. Media analysts have described this downward trend as a period of 'stagnation and decline' in the Australian press industry.[83] News proprietors at the time employed various tactics to retain readership, including lifestyle supplements, coloured lift-outs and more interactive, gamified elements such as reader competitions, jackpot lotteries and, in 1981, newspaper bingo. In fact, by November 1981, 'Mirror Bingo' and the 'Big Race Guide(s)' had become a permanent fixture in the *Daily Mirror*, flanking the newspaper's front-page banner and in subsequent pages promising readers that the 'Magnificent Mirror Bingo could change your whole life!'.[84] Around the same time, Australian newspapers like *The Daily Telegraph* began to use commercial slogans such as 'Big Value Tele' to market their publications, and light entertainment such as cartoons began to appear in the first two pages, which news proprietors regarded as the most valuable real estate in print and generally reserved for the day's biggest news stories. The *Peanuts* cartoon even became a regular feature alongside *The Daily Telegraph*'s Chamberlain news coverage. The addition of lifestyle supplements – including *Good Weekend Magazine*, which launched in 1984 with its focus on tales of humanity – changed the style and tenor of news stories. As such, the Azaria case could be read contextually as an entertainment narrative alongside the development of more interactive, personalised and incentivised market-driven content.

This substantial redefinition of news reporting in 1980s Australia wasn't confined to the press. While greater emphasis on entertainment-driven coverage could be traced to the sensationalised treatment of print news content with bold headlines and 'gossipy', voyeuristic or 'vulgar' stories about, for instance, the peccadilloes of philandering politicians, television was not immune from the shift to more popular styles and formats. The use of covert cameras and surprise hostile guests on talk shows were examples of the tabloid practices increasingly employed in television. Who could forget the 'secret lover reveal' formularised in talk shows hosted by Phil Donahue, Sally Jessy Raphaël and Ricki Lake?[85] In Australia, tabloid TV enjoyed its 'heyday' in the 1980s and 1990s when the likes of TV current affairs programs *Hinch* (1988–1994), *Inside Story* (1992) and the US syndicated *Hard Copy* (1989–1999) tickled the ratings.[86] A snapshot of television news coverage of the Chamberlain case points to this popular trend. Broadcast journalist Jim Brown appeared as the regular *Eyewitness News* reporter for Network Ten and the station's breakfast program, *Good Morning Australia*. Both programs devoted significant airtime to the Chamberlain story. In his report about the testimony of scientific experts who gave evidence at the Chamberlain trial in Darwin in 1982, Brown editorialises with his own interpretation of events:

> JIM BROWN: Now I wouldn't pretend to understand the nature of the scientific evidence that's been presented in this court over the last couple of days, but I think a fair interpretation of what's been going on is that Professor Boettcher says Mrs Kuhl's evidence is wrong and he's right.

> This is Jim Brown in Darwin for Eyewitness News.[87]

This kind of opinion-led reportage was characteristic of the transformation of television journalism in the 1980s that Graeme Turner captured so succinctly in his landmark research of the medium:

> There has been a shift away from politics and towards crime, away from the daily news agenda towards editorially generated items promoted days in advance, away from information-based treatments of social issues and towards entertaining stories on lifestyles and celebrities – and an overwhelming investment in the power of the visual, in the news as an entertaining spectacle.[88]

While once the domain of tabloids, these popular practices, formats and treatments leached into newspaper and television outlets that had carved their reputations in objective and responsible or 'quality' journalism. Where it concerns the Chamberlain case, such changes shaped the way the story was being reported in the 1980s. Even today, there is continued hand-wringing about the threat tabloidisation poses to informed and critical public debate in media and the consequent impoverishment of news and 'dumbing down' of society.[89] Yet, tabloidisation is a fraught term based on matters of taste (or subjective quality indicators) that have for hundreds of years lauded the works of, say, Shakespeare, Beethoven and Joyce and relegated the likes of Snoop Dogg, Bananarama and James Patterson to the discount bins. These judgments divide the field of popular culture into good and bad and suggest there are inappropriate uses of texts and illegitimate audience engagements with those texts (in the context of news, for example, it's okay to be an online subscriber to *The New York Times* because of its quality journalism but not the UK's *Daily Mail*).

These value systems are particularly problematic because of the gendering of popular genres and the historical association of women with 'downgraded' cultural products. Historically, hard news, such as public affairs, politics and war, has been associated with men;[90] whereas soft news or emotionally laden 'therapy news'[91] has been associated with women and confined to topics such as 'human interest, consumer news, culture and social policy'.[92] For several decades, media scholars have challenged these presumptions by arguing that soft news accords with women's lives, leads to the 'opening up' of public debate,[93] and improves audience access to abstract and complex issues.[94]

News coverage of the Chamberlain case gives us insight into the intensification of forms of popular culture in the 1980s, the commercialisation of news industries at the time, and a unique perspective on the landscape of contemporary Australian journalism as we know it today. In the next chapter, I will examine early forms of media-audience interactivity – now a hallmark of digital journalism – that challenged official legal narratives about the Chamberlains' guilt and put into question the much-accepted trial by media thesis. I will also consider the anti-social elements of public participation in this case as a rehearsal of the trolling behaviours so ubiquitous in online media today.

CHAPTER 2

TROLLING BEFORE TWITTER

> Q. What runs 'round Ayers Rock on its back legs with its arms in the air?
> A. A dingo doing a victory lap.[1]

The Chamberlains were plagued by disappointment. In 1982 the Supreme Court in Darwin convicted Lindy for murder and her husband, Michael, as an accessory after the fact. Lindy was sentenced to life in prison and the couple's subsequent appeals to the Federal and High Courts were dismissed. By all accounts, the gavel had sounded, the case had closed and Lindy would languish in prison for the term of her natural life, guilty as charged. If you called Australia home at this time, you'd likely remember the 'Top 40 Hits' of a decade that critics argued 'good music' forgot. They were inspired by the likes of Meatloaf, 'You took the baby right out of my mouth', Elvis 'You Ain't Nothin' But a Dingo Dog', and Daddy Cool 'The Dingo Rock' (See Figure 2.1).[2] Then there were the tasteless dingo jokes:

> Q. What's worse than a bull in a China shop?
> A. A dingo in a tent.
>
> Q. What were two dingoes arguing about outside a tent?
> A. Eat in or take away.[3]

The Chamberlain case even spawned various stand-up comedy routines. Radio personality Wendy Harmer's popular comedy skit adapted a song called 'Everyone Knows It's Windy' to capture the prevailing sentiment of the time: 'Everyone Knows It's Lindy'. It was a performance Harmer deeply regretted, prompting a public apology 32 years later.[4] And who could forget the caustic ballad 'Ode to Azaria' (see Figure 2.2) sung to the tune of Australia's unofficial national anthem 'Waltzing Matilda'? (NB For fans of Darryl Braithwaite, let's just say 'Wild Horses' is the other unofficial anthem). The Azaria rendition of the song staged a modern contest between Lindy and the dingo, recasting anti-establishment sentiments of the 1890s. Portrayed as an 'underdog', not unlike the slinking 'thief' of early news coverage analysed in Chapter 1, the dingo of the song symbolises the marginalised and disadvantaged in society or those caught 'against the odds'. One justification for these jokes, according to Chamberlain scholar Graham Seal, was the persistent belief Lindy and Michael had got away with murder. These feelings grew in intensity during the first inquest in 1981 and then, later, at the Supreme Court trial in 1982 when the Chamberlains were found guilty. Even today 'the dingo ate my baby' punchline persists. When actor/model/singer Paris Jackson, daughter of the late pop star Michael Jackson, visited a wildlife sanctuary on Hamilton Island, she captioned a snap on her Instagram story 'a dingo ate my baby'.[5] Paris would later offer 'sincerest apologies' for the gaffe, exclaiming she thought she was referencing an Internet meme and had no idea the phrase belonged to a tragic event in Australia's history. That's not so surprising given 'the dingo ate the baby' is now a board game described as 'a variant on rock, paper, scissors',[6] 'Dingoes ate my baby' is the name of an amateur rock band in the TV series *Buffy the Vampire Slayer*, and variations of the phrase have appeared on mugs and car bumper stickers. According to the Urban Dictionary, 'the dingo ate my baby' is even a euphemistic expression for abortion, and any cursory Google search will reveal it's used as fodder for hungry trolls too.

Trolling has a history that pre-dates the phalanx of keyboard warriors stomping their digital footprint on Instagram and Twitter. Indeed, the sometimes ignorant, cruel and often

TOP 20 HITS

	Song	Artist
1.	On the Prowl	5501' Dingos
2.	Hopelessly Devoured by You	Azaria Newton-John
3.	Come on Baby Light My Fire	Dingo Feliciano
4.	Torn Between Two Dingos	Azaria Chamberlain
5.	Breakfast in the Rock	Dingo Tramp
6.	Stop Draggin' My Baby Around	Linda Nicks
7.	Don't Let the Dingo Go Down on Me	Elton Chamberlain
8.	I Hate the Baby	John-Paul Dingo
9.	You Took the Baby Right Out of my Mouth	Dingo Loaf
10.	You Can't Stop the Dingo	The Village Babies
11.	Tent of the Rising Sun	Eric Burdon and the Dingos
12.	What's New Puppydog	The Babies
13.	How Much is that Dingo in the Window?	Tom Dingo Jones
14.	It's a Heartburn	Azaria Tyler
15.	Walkin' the Baby	The Rolling Dingo
16.	Saliva and other Bruises	The Dingo Supply
17.	You Ain't Nothin' But a Dingo Dog	Elvis Chamberlain
18.	They Called it Dingo Love	(unreadable)
19.	The Dingo Rock	Baby Cool
20.	Dingo on the Run	Azaria McCartney and Wings

Figure 2.1
A parody of the Top 40 song list of the 1980s (Seal 2009: 86)

'Ode to Azaria'
(Sung to the tune of Waltzing Matilda)

Once a jolly pastor camped in a caravan
under the shade of a kurrajong tree
and he sang and he prayed as he watched the baby's bottle boil
'You'll be a seventh day adventist like me'.

Seventh day adventist, seventh day adventist,
you'll be a seventh day Adventist like me
and he sang and he prayed as he watched the baby's bottle boil
'You'll be a seventh day adventist like me'.

Down came a Lindy to snatch up Azaria
she picked up the scissors and stabbed her with glee
and she smiled as she shoved that baby in the camera bag
'It's fun being a seventh day adventist like me'.

Seventh day adventist, seventh day adventist
It's fun being a seventh day adventist like me
And she smiled as she shoved that baby in the camera bag
It's fun being a seventh day adventist like me

Out came a dingo nosing around the camp fire
Lindy winked at Michael and said 'it wasn't me ...'
what happened to the baby you put into the camera bag
give it to the dingo and you'll get off scot free

Up jumped the dingo and ran past the camera bag
you'll never blame her murder on me
and Azaria's ghost may be heard as you pass by the kurrajong tree
'Mummy was the one who did away with me'

Figure 2.2
The ballad 'Ode to Azaria' was sung to the tune of Waltzing Matilda and circulated via office photocopies (Seal 1987: 75)

irreverent public reactions to Azaria's disappearance and aftermath foreshadowed anti-social behaviours that are now ubiquitous on social media. In this chapter I will be examining various forms of public participation in the Chamberlain story (that is, the good, the bad and the ugly) through separate library collections: a weighty archive of personal letters known as The Chamberlain Papers, written to Michael and (mostly) Lindy and now held at the National Library of Australia; and a swag of newsletters, pamphlets and booklets penned by Chamberlain activists and locked in a special collection at the State Library of New South Wales. According to cultural theorist Deborah Staines, The Chamberlain Papers represent 'one of the most important formations of a counter-public in the Chamberlain case'.[7] The letter writers comprised a Chamberlain counter-public because their collective belief in the couple's innocence was in stark contrast to those 'publics at large' or the dominant view of the time.[8] While Staines rightly argues that 'media coverage constituted these multiple publics', there is more to be said about how, aside from their one-way, personal correspondence with Michael and mostly Lindy, members of the public interacted with mainstream media.

The authors of the pro-Chamberlain pamphlets whose writings I was the first researcher to systematically analyse are among the counter-publics that existed in the 1980s and illustrate the important media-public dialogue taking place.

The chief aim of the pamphleteers was to 'Free Lindy' and for that purpose they courted media publicity, mobilised members of the public and agitated lawmakers and government to overturn the Chamberlain convictions. They were 'mediatised'[9] because counter-publics exist as spaces of social action that are transformed by media. For media sociologist Nick Couldry, mediatisation is critical to public protest because 'no social campaign can operate without some media presence'.[10] In the digital age, counter-publics can be found in internet chat rooms, online forums, blogger sites and various social media platforms. The most fundamental difference between these contemporary counter-publics and predecessors that formed in response to the Chamberlain trial verdict is the channel of expression or form of media technology they used. In particular, Chamberlain activists wielded a combination of traditional and emerging communications technology in pamphlets, booklets and video cassettes to platform their views. Aside from using the tools of media, these counter-publics frequently leant on sympathetic news media coverage of the case to bolster their cause. In many cases, mainstream media coverage shaped the tone and focus of the Free Lindy campaign, which calls into question claims of an overtly hostile, feral media.[11] But, firstly, let's look at another reputed savage, the internet troll, to see how public participation in the Chamberlain case can be situated in contemporary media debates about user generated content on social media.

Trolling: the Good, the Bad and the Ugly

While trolls have a long and sordid history, the word is most often used to signify a distinctly modern phenomenon. We're not talking about the mischievous cave lurkers and under-bridge dwellers of Scandinavian folklore or the children's toy figurines with diminutive bodies and starched rainbow hairdos. We're not even talking about the man Internet memes refer to as the world's biggest troll, former US President Donald Trump. Today, a troll conjures an anonymous keyboard cretin who traduces unsuspecting Internet users with his (they're typically male) stealthy provocations.[12] A more succinct definition of trolling courtesy of the aptly named Internet user 'Zerotrousers' in the online Urban Dictionary is 'The art of deliberately, cleverly, and secretly pissing people off, usually via the Internet, using dialogue'.[13] To piss people off without even trying? Well, that's just called 'happy coincidence'. Trolls appear to lurk in the digital ether and, for Judith Donath in her examination of identity and deception in online communities, internet trolling has its origins in the act of fishing:

> Trolling is where you set your fishing lines in the water and then slowly go back and forth dragging the bait and hoping for a bite. Trolling on the Net is the same concept – someone baits

> a post and then waits for the bite on the line and then enjoys the ensuing fight.[14]

As a form of provocation, trolling was originally intended to exclude 'newbies' in a particular forum or site by posting messages they may not understand or following behavioural norms and conventions with which they may not be familiar.[15] Such practices would emphasise a newbie's ignorance and outsider status thereby undermining their ability to form connections or achieve intra-group social status. Among social media researchers, trolling behaviours have been labelled anything from 'aberrant', 'anti-social' and 'destructive' to 'playful', 'provocative' and 'absurd'.[16] Contemporary examples of 'destructive' trolling are plentiful: in 2017 British singer Lily Allen was mercilessly taunted by Twitter trolls following the stillbirth of her son. That same year, British parents Kate and Gerry McCann reportedly received up to 150 abusive tweets a day from trolls trawling the Find Madeleine Campaign page that had been set up to assist in the search for their missing daughter. Other trolling behaviours comprise the playful end of the spectrum and are for the 'lulz'. 'Rickrolling' is a prank involving ginger-haired minstrel Rick Astley and his 1987 smash hit 'Never Gonna Give You Up'. Exploiting the tune's 'earworm' potential (steadfast ability to get stuck on loop in your head), the joke is to 'bait and switch' an unsuspecting

Internet user by sending them a disguised hyperlink that redirects to Astley's music video. As Rick himself tweeted on the 30th anniversary of the song's release, 'I said I was Never Gonna Give You Up. I am a man of my word'.[17]

The variety of trolling behaviours we see today is not so new. Arguably, these practices were rehearsed four decades ago in the 20,000 letters (typed and hand-written), notes and correspondence the Chamberlains received from a broad cross-section of the Australian public between 1980 and 1990. Catalogued as The Chamberlain Papers (MS9180), the National Library of Australia's collection of 70 archived boxes capture the extraordinary emotional outpouring of ordinary Australians whose varied responses to the case have 'symbolic significance' for the nation's cultural heritage.[18] While the letters are mostly apologetic, sympathetic and supportive of the Chamberlains' cause, an estimated five to ten per cent of the content is 'anonymous, negative and accusatory'.[19] Not unlike contemporary trolls who operate with a sense of impunity on social media, these anonymous provocateurs used traditional forms of media to enforce community norms and moral standards of behaviour, while casting Lindy aside as a figure of ridicule and contempt. Filed in the library's archives under the headings, 'nut', 'nasty' or 'unusual',[20] the following are excerpts from the more colourful contributions:

Lindy you should be hung up to the nearest tree
May you fry in Hell you bitch
You ought to hang your head in shame
If I was the judge I would have stung you as you [are] nothing but a murderess and not fit to have your baby ... you are a wicked bitch and your husband is't [sic] much better he should be a shame [sic] to say he is a man of God.[21]

Others took some literary largesse and wrote songs and poems that included stanzas such as these:

Up jumped the dingo and ran past the camera bag
'You'll never blame her murder on me'
And Azaria's ghost may be heard as you pass by the kurrajong tree
'Mummy was the one who did away with me'[22]

And the following, which is a poem called 'Azaria's Cry':

I gazed with an infant's smiling trust,
that was changed to shocked surprise.
And as death glazed
my dying eyes I cried–

–Why? Why must I die!
Still my restless spirit cries from my unmarked
grave,
Sighing – Why … Oh Why![23]

There is genuine anger in these letters along with a torrent of other emotions: shock, grief and incredulity. But as Chamberlain scholar Adrian Howe discovered in her pioneering and important study of The Chamberlain Papers, not all the letters were trollish. In fact, Howe argues that the archive shows a diversity of public opinion about the case in the gush of public sympathy and open-mindedness among letter writers who described themselves as 'quiet, good living people, and not cruel' responding to what was dubbed the 'trial of the century'.[24]

Many of these letter writers identified with a mother's pain at losing her child, wrongful persecution and a nation's prejudice, as if it were their own. The appearance of these sympathetic bon mots from ordinary members of the public coincided with a wellspring of advocacy groups that surfaced around the country. In 1984, organisations such as 'The Plea for Justice Committee', 'The Chamberlain Innocence Committee' and 'The National Freedom Council' formed to petition for the couple's innocence.[25] A strong network of advocate groups coalesced in every state in Australia (except the ACT), particularly in New South Wales with four branches registered in South Murwillumbah, Cooranbong, Parramatta and Wahroonga. These groups were responsible for 'encouraging media coverage, placing newspaper ads, organising rallies, display stands, collecting donations and approaching well-known citizens for support'.[26] Members often used the publicity surrounding the case to their advantage, by enlisting prominent individuals including the retired Supreme Court Judge Sir Reginald Scholl, Senator Mal Colston and renowned Australian artist Guy Boyd to make public declarations of support for the Chamberlains in radio and television appearances, and other public fora. One advocacy group that played a critical role in the Free Lindy campaign was the Chamberlain Information Service in Cooranbong, which published a serial called the *Azaria Newsletter.*

Pamphlets, Newsletters and Booklets

The *Azaria Newsletter* was a typed monthly bulletin of fifteen issues and five supplements that I was fortunate to be the first researcher to systematically analyse. Edited by Chamberlain advocate Nonie Hodgson, the newsletter could be purchased for 50 cents as a donation to the Chamberlain family to assist with legal and other costs. Readers were invited to contribute to the newsletter that sought '... to remain neutral and to provide a common ground in which various points of view may be expressed'.[27] Now stored in the dusty bowels of the Special Collections room of the State Library of New South Wales, the newsletters sit alongside other pro-Chamberlain campaign material such as writings from Chamberlain activists Veronica M Flanigan, Pastor George W Rollo and Terence O'Keeffe. There is also a self-published booklet by medical doctor Glenn Rosendahl; an out-of-print paperback written by self-appointed sleuth Phil Ward; a circular published by the Plea for Justice Committee demanding Lindy's release from prison with the slogan 'Fight for Justice, Free Lindy! No motive, no body, no depression, no weapon, no confession, no sense'; and an edited collection of witness statements called 'Justice in Jeopardy: Twelve Witnesses Speak Out' compiled by Guy Boyd.[28]

The writings contained in the collection were mostly distributed at local rallies and demonstrations in the years after Lindy's conviction. Both Guy Boyd and Phil Ward's titles could be purchased at local newsagencies from 1984, the latter for a reasonable sum of $6.95. But news agencies weren't the best distribution channel for Ward, so he took the matter into his own hands – literally – by depositing a copy of the book in every letterbox in Alice Springs. By all accounts, the amateur sleuth, who bore an uncanny resemblance to bearded TV chef Peter Russell-Clarke, was in the thrall of the dingo baby story. He'd spent 18 months and $125,000 of his own money searching for answers to the mystery. The former president of the ACT Bar Association said of him, 'In my long experience of the law, I have never seen any person so determined at his own expense to see justice done to almost a stranger'.[29] Unfortunately for Ward, his membership of the Seventh-day Adventist Church led some to dismiss as biased his claims (dubbed the 'Ding Theory') that 'Ayers Rock' locals had shot the semi-domesticated dingo responsible for Azaria's disappearance and conspired to cover it up. The other problem was a lack of supporting evidence, despite Ward's naming of the alleged conspirators. As it turned out, 'Ayers Rock' locals weren't happy with the Ding Theory and defamation proceedings soon followed. And yet, the book's controversial reception did little to dampen his enthusiasm. In 1984 Ward ran for the Northern Territory seat in the House of Representatives with the ticket 'Democrat provides vital Azaria clue' in a not-so-subtle promotion for his book. By way of incentive, one of his election pamphlets even promised to give voters 10,000 copies of the book. But the sweetener wasn't reflected in any moderate success at the polls when Ward secured just 2.1 per cent of the popular vote.[30] Nonetheless, he is regarded as a fearless crusader in pro-Chamberlain circles for his unrelenting determination to vindicate the couple even at great personal cost.

In all, the pro-Lindy pamphlets and the sympathetic letters in The Chamberlain Papers point to a formidable opposition to the Chamberlain convictions. However, there are important differences between the two public archives. The pamphleteers were modest in number, targeted a wide public audience, coordinated their messaging and were stoked by a desire to free Lindy. Letter writers in the Chamberlain Papers were spontaneous in their correspondence, varied in motivation and, most often, addressed their private letters to Lindy with the postmark 'at Ayers Rock', 'the Darwin courthouse', 'prison' or just 'Darwin'.[31] What is most interesting about the pamphleteers is the depth of their advocacy – they incited readers to act and speak out as a way of bolstering the pro-Chamberlain movement. The authors appealed to a 'widespread people' and 'thinking public'[32] who were dissatisfied with the court's ruling. They understood how their writings could contribute to the formation of a majority consensus that would eventually see the Chamberlain convictions overturned. In tone and intent, their language was unmistakable. For example, the Crown prosecution team at the Chamberlain trial was described as 'relentless in its determination to get a "guilty" verdict',[33] the legal process was challenged for having turned 'absolutely credible witnesses into unreliable mistaken dull heads',[34] the Northern Territory Police force was charged with a 'lack of objectivity',[35] and the court's utter disregard for Aboriginal testimony that supported the Chamberlains' account of events was considered contemptible. Rather than being on the periphery of legal developments in the case, these authors were able to attract the publicity they desired. For example, six weeks prior to the High Court appeal, the Chamberlains' trial solicitor received a copy of Rosendahl's booklet and pastor Rollo's pamphlet enjoyed some publicity when it was distributed on an Adventist speaking tour of Canada and the US. The sudden coherence of letter writers and demonstrators, in addition to the founding of advocacy groups in the two years after the trial verdict was handed down, suggest counter-publics were born out of 'communal dissatisfaction' with the Chamberlain trial verdicts.[36] But these counter-publics did not appear in an information desert, rather, mainstream media coverage of the case was critical to the form and shape of their protests.

The Pro-Chamberlain Push in News Media

It's a common refrain that the media displayed an overt and 'hostile response' to the Chamberlains, who endured a trial by media of epic proportions.[37] Remember the screeching car chases, the late-night stakeouts of the couple's Darwin hotel room, the press choppers circling the grounds of Avondale College or the frantic media scrums with their blinding flash bulbs capturing every flounce of Lindy's skirt? However, in the midst of this intrusive behaviour, there were journalists working for mainstream news outlets whose reportage was pivotal to the pro-Chamberlain movement and that would, eventually, turn the tide of public opinion in the couple's favour. They harked from all sections of the media and various news outlets with a roll call that included Malcolm Brown (*Sydney Morning Herald*), Kevin Childs (*The Age*), Kevin Hitchcock (Channel Ten), Mike Lester (Channel Nine), Kym Tilbrook (Adelaide *Advertiser*) and Ken Blanch (*Courier-Mail*). In that list were journalists Lindy described as 'guys [who] *could* lay straight in bed at night!'[38] In their pro-Chamberlain stance they would be later joined by *Herald* journalist Bill Hitchings and Jim Oram from *The Daily Telegraph*.[39] James Simmonds was also recognised by Chamberlain supporters as a journalist who had 'consistently remained objective and fair'.[40]

At the time of Azaria's disappearance, there were five broadcast networks in Australia: the publicly funded ABC and SBS and commercial stations Seven, Nine and Ten. Though a sparse media terrain, it was on television that one of the most influential news stories about Azaria's disappearance emerged. On 4 April 1984, Ten broadcast a news special called 'Azaria: A Question of Evidence'. It had the potential to secure the Chamberlains' freedom, as Michael wrote in a letter to his wife in prison:

> The new doco by 10 will be shown in Sydney April 4 at 8.30 [and] as far as I can ascertain, it will be

> hot. They have some fresh evidence that could well alter the balance against us – considerably. More meetings around Australia are coming up or have just occurred. Public opinion continues to change it seems.[41]

One reason for the program's success was its amiable host, the cherubic-faced Kevin Hitchcock who was a regular anchor for *Eyewitness News* and among the station's most respected current affairs journalists. He would later become the Director of News at Channel 10, Sydney, suffer a tragic diving accident and embark on a career as a motivational speaker. In the 1980s, Hitchcock often reported on the Chamberlain case developments, particularly between 5 June and 8 August 1986. That year, while locked in a media scrum at Darwin Airport in hot pursuit of an exclusive post-prison interview with Lindy, Hitchcock was surprised to hear himself apologise to her. Reflecting on that moment in a media interview more than a quarter of a century later, Hitchcock explained, 'The reason I apologised to her [Lindy] was that I'd worked out by then that, based on the evidence, she wasn't guilty'.[42] It was not only Chamberlain supporters who were persuaded by the program's compelling new evidence.

Hitchcock's TV special was a radical departure from traditional news programming of the period. Forget the staid conventional formats, the dry, monotonal delivery, the distanced objective reporter and the measured account of events: the Ten special incorporated fast-paced and highly edited sequences that would later be a feature of 1990s electronic tabloid *Hard Copy*, and come to typify tabloid television in Australia.[43] In a conversational and personal approach, Hitchcock introduced startling new evidence in the investigation:

> KEVIN HITCHCOCK: Good evening, I'm Kevin Hitchcock. I've been following the Azaria Chamberlain case for three and a half years. There's no doubt it's attracted more publicity than any other case in Australia's history. But there are some facts which up until now haven't come out. You will hear this information from the witnesses themselves. Most of them witnesses from the Crown prosecution. Some of them believe the Chamberlains are innocent, some are undecided but not one is convinced that the Chamberlains are guilty and all believe that in the various police and legal processes which led to the Chamberlains being convicted things occurred which should not occur in a system of democratic justice. They're speaking out because they believe the Chamberlains didn't get a fair

> hearing. The least we can do is give them one. Their unusual decision to make their views public has prompted Michael Chamberlain to give his first interview in almost three years.[44]

Pamphleteers used Hitchcock's exclusive interview with witnesses to further the Free Lindy campaign. Their persistent references to the program suggest an important dialogue was taking place between traditional news media and the pro-Chamberlain counter-publics. In her pamphlet, Veronica M Flanigan even applauded sections of the media for turning the tide of public opinion in their favour:

> Unease continues over the case, and ongoing investigations by the media have contributed to this, as vital evidence continues to emerge. Kevin Hitchcock of Channel Ten, for instance, has revealed some very convincing evidence that a dingo took the baby.[45]

The Hitchcock program is singled out several times for its contribution to the innocence campaign:

> In his TV documentary, Azaria: A Question of Evidence, Kevin Hitchcock of Channel Ten

> uncovers evidence not presented at the trial. He says that most people who appeared on the programme did so reluctantly, but they did so because they were disturbed at the handling of the case by the police, and that they had not been able to present their evidence as fully as it should have been presented to the court ...[46]

Other pamphleteers described the importance of media coverage in galvanising the pro-Chamberlain movement. In his booklet *The Dark Side of the Law* (1984), Glenn Rosendahl also refers to the Hitchcock television documentary. While questioning the trial prosecutor's claims that the Chamberlains' car contained foetal blood likely to be Azaria's, Rosendahl wrote:

> Much of this evidence (that which did not arise in court because it was unknown to the defence) has since been made public by those witnesses in the television documentary Azaria: A Question of Evidence, by Hitchcock.[47]

Even in the National Library's Chamberlain collection, correspondents claimed the Network Ten broadcast inspired them to write to Lindy, as one chirped '... Kevin Hitchcock's wonderful programme this week, A Question of Evidence, should now be shown on every channel at the same time in prime time. Not one of the many fools in our population should be allowed to miss it'.[48]

Advancements in satellite technology around this time strengthened the Chamberlain counter-publics. Firstly, conventional lag times in television broadcasts were reduced, enabling inter-state audiences to watch the Hitchcock documentary simultaneously. This meant supporters could participate in during- and post-viewing discussion about the program. Secondly, should they have missed the broadcast, copies were available for general purchase on VHS or Betamax from the Azaria Information Service. Those who purchased the *Azaria Newsletter* were encouraged to distribute copies to their local sitting members in the call to arms, 'We urge you to approach your Senators to see if they would like to view the video: "Azaria, A Question of Evidence", locally, while they are in recess'.[49] At this time, the video cassette recorder (VCR) was still new in Australia, having been commercially released in 1980 – the year of Azaria's disappearance. The technology became 'the biggest innovation in home entertainment since the introduction of the television itself', and domestic consumers were only just realising its potential as a distribution tool.[50] Creating and selling bootleg copies of the Hitchcock broadcast gave supporters a bigger audience reach while the program also legitimated their claims about the couple's innocence because a mainstream media-led investigation had unearthed potentially exonerating evidence. In all, by using emerging media technologies for distribution purposes, the Chamberlain counter-publics could coordinate their opposition, reach a wider audience and find a support base in high-profile individuals who might champion the cause.

In addition to the Hitchcock program, pamphleteers relied on a slew of news reports to legitimise their cause. Using an article from *The Australian* newspaper published in June 1984, author Terence O'Keeffe, in his 16-page pamphlet *The Dingo Shakes its Head* (1984), described how recent psychological examinations showed Lindy to be in the category of persons least likely to commit murder.[51] Similarly, Flanigan cited an article published by the *Darwin Weekend Star* in September 1983 describing Lindy as a model prisoner, and another, published in the Perth *Daily News* in April 1984, reporting the unlikelihood of Lindy having murdered her daughter.[52] Several times Flanigan attributed wider questioning of the guilty verdict to news coverage. She even observed journalists welling with emotion when the jury's findings were announced in court: 'And some of them [the media] also wept when the verdict was given – because they had just witnessed a callous miscarriage of justice'.[53] The media, Flanigan claimed, exhibited a 'level of awareness … higher than that of the jury' because of their commitment to reporting facts.[54] On another occasion, the Chamberlain activist argued media revelations about the behaviour of Northern Territory police – who 'discarded, discredited and ignored vital evidence helpful to the defence … in an effort to compel [witnesses] to change their evidence in favour of the Crown' – fortified the Free Lindy campaign.[55] As their writings make clear, activists Flanigan, O'Keeffe and Rosendahl relied on favourable media coverage to strengthen their claims the Chamberlains suffered a terrible miscarriage of justice.

There were also media personalities whose public advocacy for the Chamberlains during Lindy's incarceration was celebrated by supporters. Ita Buttrose, who was editor of *The Australian Women's Weekly* magazine at the time, was singled out for her role in shifting public views about the Chamberlains' guilt. In the *Azaria Newsletter* she is identified as a central figure in the pro-Chamberlain push:

> Australia-wide coverage in newspapers and magazines, including Woman's Day and New Idea, have given new impetus toward total exoneration. Ita Buttrose (Australia's leading woman journalist, and a celebrated 'editor-in-chief') has embraced this tragedy with a sensitive and perceptive report on the personal aspects of the Chamberlains' plight. These interviews,

> extended over 4 day [sic] with front page headline coverage in The Sun and other major syndicated papers. Ita's refreshing, honest and incisive conclusions reflect another turning point in the media's attitudes and evaluations of the case. She remarked that, like many people in Australia, she believed it possible that Lindy Chamberlain could have murdered her daughter. Now, after having talked with Michael Chamberlain and having read the new evidence and opinions collected by the Chamberlain Innocence Committee, she believes there is sufficient doubt about the case to support the call for an Inquiry.[56]

Women's magazines are credited with having provided 'new impetus' for the Chamberlains' exoneration, with *Woman's Day* and *New Idea* lauded for their responsible coverage, as will be explored further in Chapter 3. Rather than mere coincidence, references made to the media in pamphlets, booklets and newsletters amounted to a significant media-public dialogue.

In the staple of Sydney newspapers, *The Daily Telegraph* was among the first to report public unease about the Chamberlain convictions. This included news coverage of public petitions to free Lindy and reports from the Chamberlain defence team that the trial 'judge erred'.[57] Regional newspapers also gave publicity to the growing advocacy movement. *The Illawarra Mercury* newspaper issued a glowing review of Phil Ward's *Azaria: What the jury were not told* (1984), which was dubbed a 'classic whodunit', 'compulsory reading' and containing 'more allegations than you would hear in a month of NSW parliament sittings'.[58] In addition to reports questioning the guilty verdict, journalists publicly censured those in their own ranks for unseemly conduct towards the Chamberlains. Colleagues of *The Sun*'s Steve Brien, the author of the book *Azaria: The Trial of the Century* (1984), criticised the journalist for treating the couple as 'public property' and using questionable tactics to secure a story including 'ambushes, stakeouts, cat and mouse games and car chases'.[59]

Journalist and barrister John Bryson, whose book *Evil Angels* (1985) marked a turning point in public opinion about the Chamberlains' guilt (and would later inspire a Hollywood movie released in the US as *A Cry in the Dark*), wrote a scathing article for *The Age* about the media's misreporting of facts that resembled an 'inquisition'.[60] He too, was among their reporterly ranks and more recently included in an esteemed list of 'The 100 journalists of the century'.[61] In some of the letters to Lindy contained in the National Library's archive, Bryson's book was described as the inspiration for the authors' writing.[62] So too in academic circles Chamberlain scholar Adrian Howe attributes to Bryson's book her late 'conversion to the Chamberlain cause'.[63] Even

Fairfax, the former proprietors of Australia's oldest newspaper *The Sydney Morning Herald*, capitalised on the popularity of Bryson's book by purchasing prepublication rights to the title and serialising three large extracts in its stable of newspapers.[64] The extracts highlighted, among other things, the instability of the Crown case against Michael and Lindy, news coverage of the disappearance, and the often 'symbiotic' relationship between journalists and investigating police in Alice Springs.[65] While *The Sydney Morning Herald*'s publication of extracts from Bryson's book might have been self-serving, the publicity given to a text critical of Australia's news organisations, combined with the censure of journalists by prominent colleagues, emphasised the shifting and sometimes contradictory views presented by the media. For Bryson, who reflected on the case years later in an interview with *Griffith Review*, the media were not the only public institution at fault but, importantly, its members were the first to right the wrongs of the past:

> Of all the six culpable professions here – politics, media, police, law, forensic science – media was the first to change its stance to accord with the facts [sic]. And other blameworthy forces should not be protected from view. The Chamberlain case casts incidental light on the way a handful of lawyers from other states were able to occupy

politics and authority in the NT, then do as they wished with it.[66]

The issue of culpability often divides researchers of the Chamberlain case, with each anniversary a time to revisit, remember and better understand a case that has gripped the nation for over 40 years. As a consequence of this protracted navel gazing, and based on Adrian Howe's analysis of letters in archives at the National Library of Australia, we are urged to 'celebrate the people who were not caught up in the wave of media-driven hysteria'.[67] But Howe has held steadfastly to her dim view of the media since 1989 when in a provocative essay she demanded 'the media be put on trial for murder'.[68] Ultimately, she says, responsibility for the persecution of the Chamberlains rests with the 'fervid imagining of a sensationalising, unscrupulous and frequently misogynous media', not the Australian public.[69] So the media remain a masked villain, a feral figure in the hunt to attribute blame for the injustices the Chamberlains endured. But the sheer proliferation of mediatised counter-publics between 1982 and 1984 – the spontaneous letter writers and pamphleteer-penning activists who thought the guilty verdict unjust – stands as evidence of an important dialogue between everyday citizens and news media. For this reason, it's difficult to embrace a now 'kinder, gentler and more compassionate nation' in the correspondents who wrote to Lindy to express their grief and sorrow,[70] and not reconsider the role of the media too. After all, they can't be so neatly divided. As Australian media scholar and author Catharine Lumby put it so succinctly, '… how do you attack the media without attacking its consumers? Where, in other words, does the circle of production and consumption end?'[71]

Positive interaction between Chamberlain supporters and mainstream news outlets suggests two things: one, not all news hacks were hostile to the Chamberlains' bid for innocence; and, two, that Chamberlain support groups were galvanised by media coverage that called into question the official legal finding on Azaria's disappearance. As well as favourable media coverage of the case, Chamberlain supporters used new media technology such as the VHS to reach both ordinary members of the public and high-profile individuals to petition their cause. Engaging with the tools of media they disseminated their views in much the same way that Internet users voice their opinions on social media platforms today. The Chamberlain case coincided with advancements in communication, cable and satellite technologies that were increasingly mediating people's lives and fundamentally altering relationships between media producers and consumers. In the following chapter I will trace those changes further via a celebrity system that produced a media elder stateswoman out of a small-town pastor's wife.

CHAPTER 3

CELEBRITY BEFORE INSTAGRAM

> [It is] ... a case that caught the interest of the nation and inspired a small industry of books and films. So intense has been the attention paid to Mr and Mrs Chamberlain that they now deal with the media through an agent and often demand payment before talking.[1]

On the mobile photo-sharing application Instagram, the hashtags #dingoatemybaby #lindychamberlain #Azaria and #dingo reveal a colourful array of images of ordinary people tapping into the dingo baby story and the woman at its centre. In one photograph, a couple wearing oversized sunglasses, shift dresses and black bowl-cut wigs poses for the camera: the young man holds up a decapitated doll's head while the woman standing next to him thrusts in front of the camera a baby's white jumpsuit with a red-stained collar. Another photo shows a couple celebrating Halloween with a pumpkin hat, Lindy wig, bottles of beer and a sign that reads 'A dingo ate my baby!' Some post pics of souvenirs such as a baby's singlet printed with the words 'dingo bait' hanging in a stall at the Mindil Beach Night Market. Another Instagram user posts a photo of a Nevada license plate that reads DINGO 8: My Baby. Still others connect to the case through its many cultural productions: one user posts a selfie outside Alana Valentine's Letters to Lindy play, while another proudly displays copies of the newly released children's picture book *Azaria: A True History*. As these examples suggest, social media has opened up 'spaces of visibility'[2] for people outside of traditional media channels to communicate with others across distances, and it is often the means by which everyday users connect with celebrities in contemporary digital culture.

While it's now commonplace to see everyday people document their lives in front of cameras, parading perfected pouts in highly curated Instagram-worthy settings, that wasn't always the case. The lives of ordinary people weren't always so titillating. Lindy Chamberlain showed us that star-quality is not just the domain of anointed actors, models, entertainers and elite sporting figures. Her elevation to the heralded halls of fame coincided with fundamental changes to the media industry and cultural production in Australia. This chapter will trace those developments along with the emergence of a modern system of public relations to support the fame industry. The shifting style of mass-market women's magazines such as *The Australian Women's Weekly* will also be a focus, given that their colourful glossy pages increasingly embraced the intimate and personal lives of celebrities like Lindy. Whether it was in interviews detailing her prison diet, dramatic weight loss, family life and, later, marital troubles, Lindy became a vehicle for the discussion of social issues in mass-market women's magazines. Those same magazines also played a critical role in vindicating Lindy in the eyes of the broader Australian community.[3] Consequently, this chapter will consider the processes by which Lindy Chamberlain became a celebrity – in the modern sense of the word – through the manufacture of her public image, and how she was, at times, able to use the media for her own ends. Now the savvy agent of her own public persona,[4] Lindy's dealings with the media following her release from prison capture the sophisticated and complicated interactions between Australia's most wanted woman and the journalists who pursued her.

Defining Celebrity

In February 1986, Australians tuned in to hear breaking news that Lindy Chamberlain had been released from Darwin

Prison after the discovery of Azaria's matinee jacket at the base of 'Ayers Rock'. The week before, police had been combing the site in search of the remains of missing British tourist David James Brett who had fallen to his death while climbing 'the Rock'. It was then that police stumbled across the now motley, blood-stained jacket – a garment Lindy had long insisted the infant was wearing the night she disappeared and a key piece of evidence in the Crown prosecution's case against her. This discovery, nearly six years after Azaria's disappearance, proved Lindy had been telling the truth all along. Combined with the agitations of Chamberlain support groups and the publication of John Bryson's book *Evil Angels* (1985), which shook the credibility of the Crown's forensic case and captured the magnitude of injustice, it appeared the tide of public opinion had finally turned in the Chamberlains' favour. In the end, it was a journalist who played a key role in Lindy's release. Frank Alcorta from *The Northern Territory News* was tipped off about the discovery of the matinee jacket, which, despite its potential to exonerate the Chamberlains, had been held under lock and key in the Alice Springs Courthouse for nearly a week. He threatened to go public with the story if Lindy was not released or an inquiry announced. The government did both.[5]

In the publicity-filled days and weeks that followed Lindy's shock prison release, competition among media outlets for her exclusive prison story reached fever pitch and it was the most coveted scoop in Australia. By 1986, Lindy had well and truly shirked her cloak of ordinariness and entered the celebrity stratosphere. In many ways, Lindy fulfilled the criteria of modern celebrity. She wasn't famous for a particular skill or achievement, lauded for her moral worth or of noble birth or lineage. These were the necessary attributes for public recognition in the 17th and 18th centuries when, as Canadian media scholar P David Marshall describes in his book *Celebrity and Power* (1997), fame was the domain of 'great men', heroic figures and clergymen. By the mid-19th century, however, celebrity began to be associated with vulgarity and inauthenticity and the term itself was used in a derogatory manner to refer to a fleeting and superficial condition.[6] It is from this tradition that we derive Daniel Boorstin's famous definition of celebrity being a person who is 'well-known for their well-knownness'.[7] In the 20th century, the 'public personality' emerged alongside the 'democratic myth' of his or her celebrity achievement as a result of a new democratic age in which class no longer predetermined the course of one's destiny.[8] At this time, celebrity became an 'ideal representation of the triumph of the masses' and a condition that could be celebrated and shared.[9] The concept of celebrity as democratic ideal originates in the Latin term *celebrem*, which implies being well-known and 'thronged' by the public, as Marshall explains:

> The celebrity, in this sense, is not distant but attainable – touchable by the multitude. The greatness of the celebrity is something that can be shared and, in essence, celebrated loudly and with a touch of vulgar pride. It is the ideal representation of the masses.[10]

Without the restrictions of hierarchical systems of old, modern celebrity was an attainable quality associated with the triumph of the masses. As such, celebrity became dependent on the availability of the famous individual who had direct contact with the public. On the face of it, the social media hashtags #dingoatemybaby #lindychamberlain #Azaria and #dingo provide comic relief and document a moment in time – whether that's attending a Halloween party in a Lindy wig photographing a 'dingo bait' baby's singlet at a night market or posing in front of signage at a Lindy stage play. But more than that, these digitally mediated intimacies offer the possibility of connection with a woman who is now a peerless icon in Australian cultural history.

Back in the 1980s Lindy was no garden-variety celebrity plucked from a fashion shoot or casting call. Neither was she one of the multiskilled 'slashies' (actor-slash-model-slash-whatever) whose dazzling smiles are broadcast on Instagram Stories and for whom social media is a virtual pulpit to proselytise about health and wellness. These fame-seeking fixtures in our social media feeds are part of the rank and file of 21st century 'microcelebrities' who, according to digital media scholar Theresa Senft, boost their popularity through a new style of online performance on video, blogs and social networking sites.[11] Lindy doesn't fit the 'microcelebrity' tag and her public profile sits uneasily in the pantheon of celebrity types identified in leading studies of the phenomenon. According to Chris Rojek in his landmark study *Celebrity* (2001), there are four primary categories of celebrity: 'ascribed celebrity' based on biological destiny or lineage (think: Prince William); 'achieved celebrity', which derives from an individual's accomplishment or skill (think: Usain Bolt); 'attributed celebrity', which is the celebrity whose fame has been manufactured by PR and promotional industries (think: Kim Kardashian); and the 'celetoid' who barely registers a blip on the fame radar as a reality television star, lottery winner or one-hit wonder (apologies to The Knack for the unedifying mention here).[12] Rather than celetoid, other celebrity scholars use the terms 'accidental celebrity' and 'accidental hero' to refer to an unremarkable celebrity existence, the passing fad type of fame.[13] But Lindy's is not a fleeting face in the annals of history and the circumstances of her celebrity are no cause for celebration.[14] Rather, her fame is perched on 'unfavourable public recognition' as a woman once convicted and now exonerated of murder.[15] Thrust into the media spotlight in August 1980, she has remained in that glaring gaze ever since.

There were major shifts in the Australian media industry and cultural production in the 1980s that give insight into Lindy's prominent status and, in a wider sense, the growing public appetite for celebrity culture. A number of local film projects and their leading actors had been successfully marketed internationally at this time, including *Mad Max* (1979) and its sequel *Mad Max 2* (1981); *The Man from Snowy River* (1982) and *Crocodile Dundee* (1986). In the same decade, locally produced television soap operas *Neighbours* (1985) and *Home and Away* (1988) were garnering a young audience of fans.[16] The emergence of a local celebrity industry and the growing marketability of Australia's roll call of famous faces (Mel Gibson, Paul Hogan and Molly Meldrum) also meant less reliance on British and American imports to fill the pages and screens of local markets.[17] Growth in the domestic entertainment industry also spawned a cluster of public relations, publicity and marketing agencies that shaped Australian media content in the 1980s.[18]

Internationally, the public relations industry has a colourful history. In the US its origins can be traced to the late 19th and early 20th centuries when entrepreneur and showman PT Barnum staged a number of spectacular performances in New York to draw attention to his American Museum filled with freak shows, wax works and flea circuses.[19] Australia's public relations industry has a more recent history. In the 1930s, journalist George William Sydney Fitzpatrick placed an advertisement in the telephone book marketing himself as a 'registered practitioner in public persuasion, propaganda, publicity'.[20] He has since been credited as Australia's first public relations practitioner.[21] The subsequent founding in 1949 of the Sydney-based Australian Institute of Public Relations has been 'regarded as the official start of public relations as a profession in Australia'.[22] Industry pioneers of the period created a blueprint for today's publicity industry by marketing innovative events to attract maximum public interest.[23] But it was in the 1980s that Australia's public relations industry intensified, as did ethical debate about the practice of chequebook journalism, fuelled by intense competition for Lindy's first post-prison interview.

Chequebook Journalism and PR

On Lindy's release in 1986, news media outlets jostled to be the first to report her prison ordeal, extreme weight loss and reunion with family and friends. A year earlier, *The Bulletin* magazine had predicted the value of Lindy's story: 'Lindy Chamberlain has a story to tell and the telling is going to cost a lot of money'.[24] In the end, Australian Consolidated Press (ACP) secured the deal after settling on the figure of $250,000 for an interview with the Chamberlains on their current affairs program *60 Minutes* and in the popular monthly magazine *The Australian Women's Weekly*. One observer noted, even though it was nothing new for the media to pay for stories, '... when Lindy Chamberlain was released from Darwin prison in February 1986, chequebook journalism took on a whole new dimension'.[25] Agent to the stars Harry M Miller was at the forefront of Australia's promotions industry, so it was no surprise he got the Chamberlain gig. Between 1980 and 1994, Miller brokered three interviews for the Chamberlains on *60 Minutes*.[26] The first was a highly publicised deal and not without controversy, as signalled in the epigraph to this chapter. According to *Time* magazine, journalists who criticised the couple for selling their story were hypocrites as indicated in comments such as: '... for some of its most notorious practitioners to use the deal to snipe at the Chamberlains is rich'.[27] Satirising the media hype the Chamberlain deal generated, *The Bulletin*'s Mark Cornwall depicted in cartoon a dingo with flashy sunglasses and microphone standing in front of 'Ayers Rock'. The caption read 'You've decided to confess?' The dingo replies 'I always wanted to meet Mike Willesee'[28] (see Figure 3.1).

The exclusive *60 Minutes* interview with the Chamberlains was broadcast on 2 March 1986. It was the culmination of five separate meetings between the Chamberlains and host Ray Martin, who spent time with the family and recorded a reunion service held in their honour at the Seventh-day Adventist

Church in Cooranbong. So hotly anticipated was the story that the program's lengthy pre-broadcast publicity led audiences to tune into the wrong segment:

> The week preceding [the Chamberlains' interview] 60 Minutes ran a profile of the cricketer Greg Matthews. Many viewers must have thought the Chamberlains were on. In the Sydney market 60 Minutes rated 43, an unheard of figure even for a popular sporting figure. Next week, when the first Chamberlain interview was broadcast, it rated 42 in Sydney and 50 in Melbourne. 60 Minutes ran a second interview the following week with equally spectacular results.[29]

Scheduling problems aside, the program highlighted the great level of interest in Lindy's story, particularly at the point where Ray Martin (RM), playing devil's advocate, interrogated Lindy (LC) in what became one of television's most frequently quoted exchanges:

> RM: Well, let me ask you face-to-face what every Australian would ask you: did you kill Azaria?
> LC: No way. I loved that little girl.[30]

To squeeze the moment of pathos, the camera zoomed in to reveal a close-up shot of Lindy's welling eyes and broken facial expression as she answered the question. In front of television sets all around the country, people leaned into the exchange. *The Daily Telegraph* cartoonist Paul Zanetti parodied the moment in an illustration of two 'arm-chair judges' in wig and gown, perched on living room chairs watching Lindy Chamberlain on the television screen (Figure 3.2). Martin's interview then cut to an intimate scene of Lindy, in white summer dress, playfully lifting and swinging her toddler Kahlia by the arms, unwittingly revealing the mother's matching knickers underneath. In his line of questioning, Martin also probed Lindy's heartbreaking offer to Michael to end their marriage so that he could start a new life while she was in prison. Lindy responded:

> LC: You think of your children needing comfort and your husband needing comfort and there's just no one there, you're powerless to do anything and consequently, if that meant me fading out of the picture I was prepared to do it even though I didn't want to …[31]

The program's intimate portrayal of private heartbreak, familial bonds and familiar hardships appeared to soften Lindy's public image. In response to the interview, one man wrote a letter to Lindy giving his 'overall impression' of the reasons why the public were initially hostile towards her: 'most people in Australia were not prepared to accept that a woman could respond rationally, eloquently and calmly in stressful circumstances'.[32]

Ray Martin's interview signalled a radical departure from the 'formal, modern and paternalistic' approach of current affairs journalism in the 1960s.[33] At this time, program hosts favoured a stiff approach, detached delivery and ponderous pieces-to-camera.[34] By contrast, Martin took us into the private world of his interviewees, gave us a warm and personality-driven style of delivery and, that approach, contributed to his standing as a pivotal figure in the transformation of Australian current affairs journalism.[35] Alongside George Negus, Jana Wendt and Michael Willesee in the dome of news celebrities in the 1980s, Martin spoke the common vernacular, appealed to his audience and embodied the solid reputation of the Nine Network steered by the Packer dynasty – all crucial factors in his career success.[36] Under Martin, the program used narrative voiceovers, bold typeface and rapid editing sequences that were becoming a staple of current affairs journalism of the period.[37] The tabloidese style and format of programs such as *60 Minutes* were most pronounced during the 'halcyon days' of current affairs television in the late 1980s and early 1990s. At this time, perpetually outraged host Derryn Hinch dominated the coveted 7 pm national timeslot with his week-nightly current affairs program *Hinch* (1987)[38] boasting up to two million viewers per night. Memorable segments included the 'shame file' on drink drivers and the 'sludge file' on people dumping sump oil, as the shock jock Hinch fondly recalled in an interview with *Mumbrella* in 2012.[39] Similar in shouty style to Gordon Elliott's weekly hour-long *Hard Copy*, these landmark current affairs programs mirrored the highly sensationalised formula of popular print publications of the period.[40] The rise in entertainment-based consumer television and shifting audience tastes transformed the media industry and we can see some of those changes in reportage of the Chamberlain case.

Women's Magazines

As part of the Harry M Miller deal with ACP in March 1986, the Chamberlains were also interviewed for *The Australian Women's Weekly*. The magazine story provided a similarly intimate portrait of a family beset by tragedy and marked an important milestone in the public's wider acceptance of Lindy. Now half her size in weight, sporting a pixie haircut and offering readers full and frank disclosure of her life over the previous six years, Lindy was described as having 'let down her guard [in] an about-face that goes far beyond the dramatic change in her appearance'.[41] That drastically altered appearance was of 'a stranger: tiny, bird-like, sharp-featured, with a modified punk brushed-back hair style, trim waist, shapely legs with fashionable black and gold sandals, and a beaming smile'.[42] The magazine also revealed the 'feelings she hid behind a frozen mask', the 'turmoil' Lindy suffered and 'the feelings and emotions she has bottled up for so long'.[43] While critics have argued the magazine's interview with Lindy returned her 'to the fold of normalcy'[44] by recasting her in the stereotype of 'the mother' in a 'suburban family' idyll,[45] it is also possible to see the report's wider significance in establishing a connection between Lindy and the publication's largely female readership. As Catharine Lumby writes of the condition of modern celebrity, we live in 'a world where the intensity of media coverage is fuelling a public fascination with the "real" people who lurk behind the images which saturate our screens and front pages'.[46] So, it was the 'real' Lindy Chamberlain *Women's Weekly* attempted to capture in her intimate thoughts and feelings about 'common' experiences for women such as motherhood, marriage, body image, sorrow and loss. At one point in the magazine interview, Lindy's incarceration is brought into the familiar, into the realm of everyday experience:

> Jail had been Lindy's life for long enough for her to talk of it as the average housewife might talk about an extended enforced holiday in a place she

would never want to go back to.[47]

Appealing to the 'average housewife' and, more broadly, the women of Australia on such matters was no easy task, as Senator Bob Collins said at the time: 'the greatest obstacle in changing public perceptions about Lindy was the women of Australia'.[48] Yet it was in the domain of women's magazines that Lindy connected with ordinary women. The magazine interview also offered readers practical advice about weight loss using Lindy's dramatic physical transformation as an example. Lindy was reported to have followed a high-protein 'vegetarian diet' that consisted of '… egg salad and eggs and a few vegetables, and eggs, or eggs', while her strict exercise regime included 'jogging around the [prison] compound and doing exercises'.[49] The magazine described her look as 'feminine and attractive' and smiling photographs of her and husband Michael would attest to this fact.

Typically, in the 1950s women's periodicals contained short pieces of fiction, letters, recipes, columns and few illustrations. By the 1980s, as magazine coverage of the Chamberlain case illustrates, the glossies devoted significant coverage to celebrities in visually driven stories.[50] Arguably, Australian women's magazines of the period began to reconstitute themselves through major national news stories, finding in the Chamberlain case a representative woman to cultivate. Alongside 'practical knowledge', including household tips, recipes and shopping pages, women's magazines offered human interest stories that represented a form of 'connected knowledge' or 'emotional learning' enabling readers to identify with celebrities like Lindy.[51] As an example of the more democratic modern phenomenon of celebrity, Lindy was 'defined for us by her ordinariness' and more relatable to the magazine reader.[52]

Constructions of the 'Lindy' persona in media provided an opportunity for individuals to connect with a public figure whose experiences might tally with their own. The continuity of Lindy's media presence functioned in much the same way that celebrities have become immensely appealing to their audiences for the fact they are publicly 'known'.[53] There was little need to elaborate on either headlines containing the name 'Lindy' or news articles with a photograph of her beside them, since, to the Australian public, her image was so familiar. Put simply, it was enough to publish headlines such as 'Mother Killed Azaria, SM told'[54] and 'My sister Lindy: God still loves her'[55] without giving any further clues as to whose identity they belonged. Reflecting on ABC News coverage of Lindy's prison release in February 1986, one of the station's hosts, Wendy Carlisle, commented that 'When ABC Radio News reported the story, there was never any need to explain just who Lindy Chamberlain was'.[56]

Figure 3.1

Cartoonist Mark Cornwall satirised the media hype surrounding Lindy Chamberlain's exclusive post-prison interview, 26 November 1985, *The Bulletin*, p. 36 [Australian Consolidated Press]

Figure 3.2

Cartoonist Paul Zanetti depicted Ray Martin's famous interview with the Chamberlains for *60 Minutes*, complete with arm chair judges, 3 March 1986, *Daily Telegraph*, p. 20 [News Limited]

Frocks, Politics and Feminist Scholarship

From the outset, descriptions of Lindy's physical appearance were the subject of newsprint, radio talkback, current affairs programs and television broadcasts. At the second inquest, one observer noted how she wore an 'orange and purple patterned dress ... her shoulders, bare except for the thin straps of her dress, showed the pink tint of sunburn'.[57] Later that year at the Supreme Court trial, she presented a maternal figure in billowing frocks, heavily pregnant with her fourth child.[58] As *The Sun-Herald* reported: 'The Chamberlains have been tightly controlled. Mrs Chamberlain has continued her dress sense in the maternity mode. She has had a new maternity dress each day'.[59] A few weeks later at the announcement of the guilty verdict, *The Sydney Morning Herald* reported a wardrobe malfunction: 'Mrs Chamberlain, in a powder blue dress with white frills – the same dress she wore when giving evidence for the defence – sat without apparent emotion. Her husband sat beside her'.[60] Two days later, when Lindy was sent to prison, her absence did little to assuage media interest in her physical appearance. Instead, attentions turned to her 'secret childhood', where she was described as 'a beautiful little girl, so natural, a little fairy'.[61] Whether it was her choice of dress, averted gaze or guilty 'look', the public often interpreted the Chamberlain case through its principal subject.

At times, even the success of the defence case was measured against a fleeting facial expression or the dress Lindy wore to court each day. This was no more apparent than when news of the pregnancy coincided with a critical stage in the judicial process, when the trial jurors were grappling with the weight of forensic evidence.[62] Believing that she might evoke the sympathies of the jury and thwart the prosecution's hopes for a guilty verdict, media pundits referred to Lindy's condition as a 'forensic pregnancy'.[63] News coverage of Lindy's changing figure frequently became an interpretive device for readers to consider the weight of scientific evidence. For example, Malcolm Brown wrote for *The Sun-Herald*:

> Lindy Chamberlain, nearly eight months pregnant, is never comfortable. She sits and squirms all day on the special chair provided in the body of the court, sometimes putting her feet up on a little stool. Occasionally she jerks a limb or moves suddenly, responding perhaps to the kicking of the baby inside her.[64]

This kind of reportage is not unfounded given that individuals are judged on how they appear in the world of media and law: 'courts have always been forums for performing and spin-doctoring. That even in the courtroom, the real war has always been a war over representation'.[65] Lindy had clearly grown into a recognisable 'social type' – her mode of dress, weight gain, weight loss, pregnancy and prison diet were the subject of endless speculation and controversy, with Lindy herself remarking that each time the public saw her she was described as 'either pregnant or just getting over it'.[66]

Contradictory representations of Lindy Chamberlain's image were fanned in media and elsewhere. On the one hand, Lindy's femininity was alluded to in reports of her as a 'perfect mother',[67] whose sexual appeal was 'self-evident' in her 'beautiful', 'darkly vivacious good looks'.[68] At other times, Lindy refused to cry in public, appeared 'impassively' cold and disciplined and bore a masculine presence.[69] Among feminist scholars researching the Chamberlain case there has been a tendency to focus on media portrayals of Lindy as a witch. One of the reasons cited is the unnecessary media attention on her physical appearance and 'self-evident' sexuality[70] – whether in a 'filmy apricot dress' and leg-skimming 'summer frock'[71] or in reports of the 'soft roundness of her tanned shoulders', 'petite figure' and 'eye-catching frame'.[72] Also contributing to her witch-like status were accounts of Lindy's shapeshifting figure from slender at the second inquest in 1982, heavily pregnant at the trial later that year, and then 'emaciated' upon her prison release in 1986. Her post-prison body fuelled a range of reports in which she was described as a 'stranger – tiny, gaunt, wraithlike, terribly thin and brittle',[73] sporting a 'fashionable' wardrobe,[74] and even rejuvenated as the *Sunday Territorian* reported:

> The slight, five foot nothing, smiling woman that greeted my Editor Gary Shipway, and myself in the Darwin Jail last Tuesday did not look at all like Lindy Chamberlain of the inquests and trial. Gone were the hard eyes and sullen gesture, the chubby face with the petulant mouth, and the rolling gait of a woman accused of murdering her baby … Instead we were greeted by an attractive, petite and healthy woman looking much younger than her 37 years.[75]

Though Lindy's changed appearance is highly sentimentalised in this report, it is an example of shifting news media representations of her image. Far from the singing chorus or monolithic block of opinion many assume 'the media' to be – indeed, the view of a hostile and impenetrable media was the dominant analysis of the 1970s[76] – Lindy's representations reveal a chiaroscuro of contrasting portrayals. Additionally, the chronicling of celebrity physical development is nothing new, nor is it confined to women: the public act of witnessing the 'bloating, slimming, wounding and general humiliation' of celebrity bodies has a variegated history in figures such as Elvis Presley, Elizabeth Taylor, Michael Jackson and Oprah Winfrey.[77]

Reading Lindy's image through a socio-political lens provides important context in the debate about her media representations. In the two decades prior to Azaria's disappearance, second wave feminism ignited interest in the cultural and political inequalities of women that had real world impacts. In 1970 in Australia, women couldn't secure a mortgage or purchase a car without their husband or father countersigning the documents. Against this background, defining voices in western feminism emerged with the likes of Susan Brownmiller, Andrea Dworkin and Kate Millett. Local icons Germaine Greer and Anne Summers articulated the experiences and cultural peculiarities of disenfranchised women in Australia with their ground-breaking tomes *The Female Eunuch* (1970) and *Damned Whores and God's Police* (1975). Greer's witty and defiant polemic nearly sold out of its second print run in 1971 despite controversy about memorable provocations within its pages, such as 'Women have very little idea of how much men hate them'.[78] Agitations for social change rippled through the instrument of government too, with Australia's first Women's Adviser to the Prime Minister, Elizabeth Reid, appointed in 1973. It was at this time that the 'femocrat', or 'a woman, feminist by personal conviction, who works within a government bureaucracy at a senior level to advance the status of women in society',[79] pushed for gender-sensitive policies and funding for women's services.[80] The foundation of the Women's Electoral Lobby (WEL) in 1972 and Australia's first federal anti-discrimination law, the Sex Discrimination Act (1984), entrenched these social justice objectives by outlawing 'discrimination in employment, education and the provision of services on the grounds of sex, marital status or pregnancy'.[81] Other advancements in this era included Australia's ratification in 1983 of the United Nations Convention on the Elimination of All Forms of Discrimination Against Women (CEDAW), and the passing of the Affirmative Action (Equal Employment Opportunity for Women) Act 1986, which established the Affirmative Action Agency to adequately administer the provisions set out in the Act. The social and political gains of feminism in this period offer an important historical backdrop to the case and an understanding of Lindy's representations in media. Whether she appeared 'hard-faced' or 'in shock', in a 'black dress' with 'red lips'[82] or a 'floral-print sundress, bobbysocks and sneakers',[83] Lindy reflected anxieties about the performance of gender and the changing status of women at this time.

There is little doubt Lindy's media coverage was often gendered, and plentiful examples of her sexualised portrayal exist, as I have argued elsewhere.[84] However, feminist scholarly research on the Chamberlain case appears to overlook the rise and packaging of feminism as a social movement in the 1980s.[85] Feminist ideology was, in fact, being democratised and distributed through popular forms and, controversially, gaining a wide public audience. It even pervaded a range of popular women's magazines in the 1970s, with Cleo unashamedly declaring itself a feminist periodical. Thus, media outlets were not the only site of image production: ideologically, feminism was also implicated in the framing devices used in representations of the Chamberlain case and Lindy, in particular. For example, this can be seen in feminist critical analysis of a prevailing misogyny in Australian society that contributed to 'the making of Lindy the witch' and her casting as a 'martyr to her sex'.[86] Diverse interest groups fanned representations of Lindy's image in public debate across media, academic and legal circles. As such, there was no 'one' overarching interpretation of Lindy's persona but, rather, a series of competing discourses framing her image for different ends. Those differing representations gave audiences an opportunity to read her appearance in alternate and sometimes contradictory ways.

While Lindy has been the focus of a news media gaze at turns sympathetic and hostile – and controlling such representations can be a difficult task – she has shown the capacity of individuals to exploit stereotypes and use the media for their own ends. Some of the ways Lindy was able to exercise agency over her own public profile were in self-managed public appearances, the employment of public relations agent Harry M Miller, and the publication of her tell-all autobiography, *Through My Eyes* (1990). In an interview for *New Idea* magazine, Lindy was quoted as saying she '[will] never be a victim' because 'Being a victim is a choice and you aren't a victim unless you choose to be'.[87] Lindy, it appears, had an uncanny sense of her own agency in the telling of her story. Rather than a beast spitting savage and sexist views, the news media is sprawling and multifaceted, an ever-expanding site of contestation and debate and a place where contradictory views collide. However fleetingly, Lindy showed a capacity to resist, shape, alter and contest her own mediated images at a time in Australia when the status of women was shifting along with the cultural production of celebrity: newspapers transformed into mass circulation commodities, media technologies proliferated, the public sphere expanded into the domestic realm and a system of public relations developed to meet with the challenges brought about by an intense exposure of celebrity bodies. Read in relation to these changes, the Chamberlain case marks a turning point in modern consumer culture. How the reporting of Azaria's disappearance, which occurred alongside other commemorative events, tapped into processes of nation building in the 1980s, will be the focus of the next chapter.

CHAPTER 4

SORRY, NOT SORRY

> The mysticism of Ayers Rock, long recognised by Aboriginal people, was only slowly starting to filter through to other Australians. Somehow, especially to urban people, this symbol of the continent's fundamentals seemed related to Azaria's disappearance.[1]

> The new path of Australia after the fifth of March, 1983, will be national reconciliation, national recovery, national reconstruction.[2]

A cursory glance at the Twitter handle @MyFavMurder is a reminder of the deep connection between the Chamberlain story and the cultural landscape in which Azaria disappeared. One tweeter even scolded another for failing to use the correct terminology when referring to a site that is sacred to its traditional Indigenous owners:

> thanks for talking about lindy and Azaria chamberlain! just so you know, we're supposed to call it Uluru, not Ayers Rock. It's extremely sacred to Indigenous Australians and they called it Uluru before us whities bastardised it [sic].

Aside from the Azaria – 'Ayers Rock' connection, this tweet recalls a history of ambivalence to Aboriginal politics that the ABC summed up in the catchphrase 'Sorry, not sorry'.[3] As a millennial slogan, 'Sorry, not sorry' can be found in pouty and petulant memes, in shrug-shouldering gifs and in songs of defiance popularised by rockers Amen and songstress Demi Lovato. But the insincere apology has cultural significance beyond any 'my bad' wave of the hand. This is especially the case where 'Sorry, not sorry' is deployed in debates about Australia's progress towards equality and reconciliation with Indigenous Australians and acts of official remembrance at odds with contemporary political contexts.[4] In relevant academic research, the historical burden of settler Australia's past treatment of Indigenous Australians has weighed heavily on commemorative events and moments of national significance.[5] These include the passing of Aboriginal Land Rights legislation in NSW in 1983 and in the Northern Territory in 1976, the ceremonial handover of 'Ayers Rock' in 1985, the gesture of reconciliation proposed in the Barunga Statement of 1988, and the 'pomp and protests' surrounding the commemoration of 200 years since the arrival of the First Fleet of British convict ships in Sydney Harbour. In particular, the years 1982 to 1992 recorded 'major changes in Aboriginal–white relations in Australia' with a number of archaeological and historical works opening up Indigenous self-determination and sovereignty for wider public discussion, though no official apology for past injustices was forthcoming.[6] It was not until 2008 that the Australian Government issued an historic apology to Australia's Indigenous people. Four years later, Coroner Elizabeth Morris issued an apology to the Chamberlains for the personal injustices they had endured (see Conclusion).

This chapter will argue that moments of national cultural significance coincided with key developments in the Chamberlain case. Not only did the sacred Indigenous site of 'Ayers Rock' witness the infant's disappearance in 1980, but it was at its scrubby base that Azaria's matinee jacket was discovered in 1986, prompting Lindy's early release from prison. The Adelaide *Advertiser* reported years later that 'the continent's fundamentals seemed related to Azaria's disappearance' and, as argued in Chapter 1, 'Ayers Rock' became a key character in early news reports of a story 'heavy [with] symbols of Australianness', that contributed to 'its bizarre quality and widespread appeal'.[7] Subsequent attempts to memorialise the Chamberlain story in the curation of a permanent Azaria collection at the National Museum of Australia in 1988 and the release that year of the first Hollywood feature film on the subject, *Evil Angels*, often channelled wider conversations about nationhood, sovereignty and identity. Magnified by its historical relation to larger events, the case occurred at a tipping point in the renegotiation of Australian national identity, particularly in the 1980s. By analysing news coverage of the Azaria saga at this time, we are better able to understand our own development as a nation on the cusp of the 21st century.

'The Rock Back Where It Belongs'

While Lindy languished in prison serving her life sentence and support groups around the country swelled in their agitations for her release, the NSW Government passed the Aboriginal Land Rights Act (NSW) 1983, which was an attempt to repair, arrest and compensate for the dispossession of Indigenous Australians over 200 years of European occupation.[8] Earlier that year, Bob Hawke led the Australian Labor Party to a landslide victory against Malcolm Fraser's Liberal–National Coalition Government on an election platform that included land rights legislation.[9] Despite failing on its promise to pursue a treaty with Indigenous

Australians, the Hawke Government would initiate important social reforms and make progress towards the preservation of Indigenous cultural heritage sites, as the Labor Leader's election policy speech – quoted at the beginning of this chapter – mandated to do. Combined with the Fraser Government's earlier passing of the Aboriginal Land Rights (Northern Territory) Act 1976 that achieved full bipartisan support, the NSW legislation was another critical step in the recognition of Indigenous spiritual ties to country that are fundamental to their continued cultural survival. As anthropologist and Indigenous activist Marcia Langton AO told a conference in 1988, 'The present predicament of Aboriginal people is the direct historical result … of the doctrine of terra nullius, that legal fiction of British international law which justifies the total dispossession of Aboriginal people …'[10] One of the most symbolic and deeply divisive moments in the national debate about Indigenous land rights followed Hawke's announcement in November 1983 that the Aboriginal Land Rights Act would be amended to return the title for Uluru-Kata Tjuta National Park, an area encompassing 'Ayers Rock', to its traditional owners.

The historic handover ceremony hosted by the Governor-General, Sir Ninian Stephen, took place on 26 October 1985 and was decorated with international dignitaries: the British, Canadian and New Zealand High Commissions, the West German and French embassies and the High Commission of the Republic of Kenya. However, celebrations of the event were marred by 'colour and controversy'.[11] That morning, *The Sydney Morning Herald* reported 'Truckloads of Aborigines – many of them performers – on the way from Alice Springs to the Rock were harassed at service stations and handed pamphlets demanding the handover be stopped'.[12] The ceremony itself was reported as '... dusty and chaotic. Hoards of children raced blithely through the middle of proceedings'.[13] Northern Territory Chief Minister Ian Tuxworth refused to attend the ceremony and instead planned to hold a news conference denouncing the 'national tragedy' as little more than a '$400,000 sausage sizzle'.[14] In the afternoon, traditional owners of the site treated federal ministers and their partners to 'a bush-tucker hunt [which included] munching barbecued witchety grubs' that apparently Mrs Holding, the wife of the Minister for Aboriginal Affairs the Hon Clyde Holding, 'enjoyed immensely'.[15]

Whether in parliamentary debate, newspaper editorials or opinion pages, national conversation brimmed with talk about the transfer of ownership of the 'Ayers Rock' site. One of the most vocal opponents was Ian Cameron, then leader of the National Party in Queensland, who told Federal Parliament that the 'mystical' quality of 'the Rock' was for 'all of us, not just the Aborigines'.[16] Similarly, journalist John Stone argued the handing of 'Ayers Rock' to one group of Australians was 'at the expense of fellow citizens'.[17] He added:

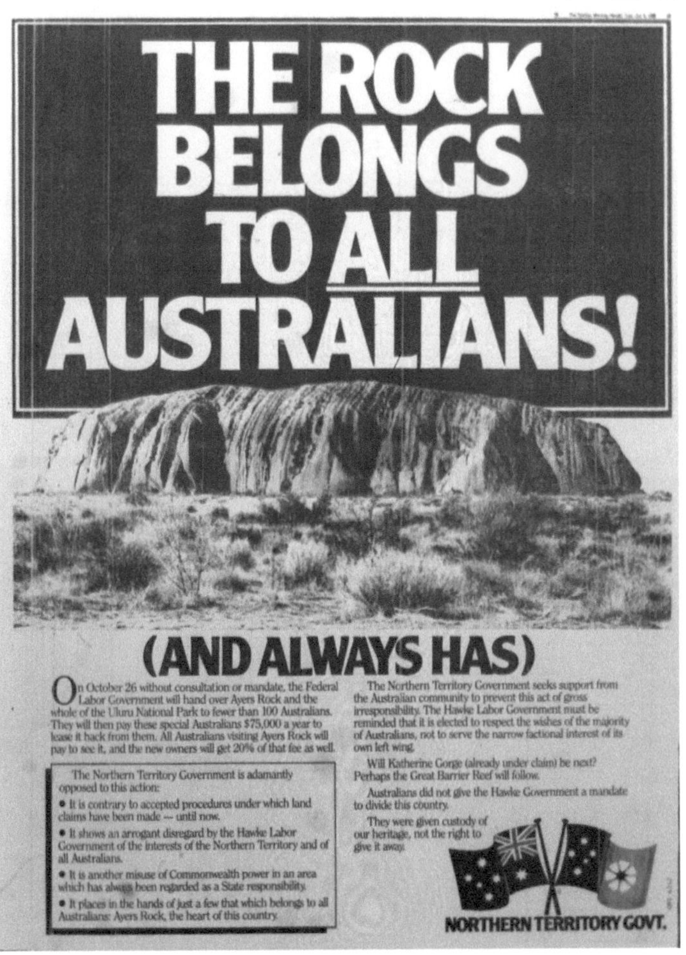

Figure 4.1

Northern Territory Government sponsored advertisement opposing the handover of 'Ayers Rock' to its original owners, 8 October 1985, *The Sydney Morning Herald*, [Fairfax]

Tuesday, November 5, 1985

LETTERS TO THE EDITOR

The Rock back where it belongs

SIR: We were disgusted with the Northern Territory Government's newspaper advertisement of October 26 regarding Mr Hawke's actions on Ayers Rock.

Mr Tuxworth says:- It no longer belongs to all Australians.

We say: It now belongs to the original owners or descendants, before it was stolen, vandalised and capitalised upon by white invaders.

He says: The Hawke Government will give Ayers Rock away to fewer than 100 Australians.

We say: Why are there so few owners left? The result of a slow process of genocide? But of course that's debatable among a few.

Also, those 100 Australians are more capable of ensuring the heritage and sacredness of this site than any white people could imagine. It is their heritage and their culture. For whites it is exploitable real estate and a conveniently adapted heritage.

He says: They will get $75,000 a year.

We say: $75,000 for 100 people works out at $750 a person – way below the poverty line (park rangers get more than $750 a year). Also, 20 per cent of all fees is piddling. The Government will get the other 80 per cent – isn't this a bit exorbitant for rates?

He says: Australians will have to pay to visit the rock in future.

We say: If it were white people who owned the rock and charged visitors' fees, no-one would comment. Why then begrudge Aborigines charging? That smells of double standards.

He says: The Hawke Government is dividing the country.

We say: Hawke is contributing to the restoration of land to the original owners. Just because white men have divided this country recklessly and sold it to foreign ownership, etc, for 200 years, does not make it morally right.

Hawke has not given Australian land away. He has returned Australian land to the rightful owners. Congratulations, Mr Hawke, we support you.

Mum Shirl, J. George and friends of the Redfern Community,
Redfern Street,
Redfern.
October 30

Ugly Australians

SIR: I would like to take this opportunity to thank Mr Tuxworth for his most edifying performance at Ayers Rock. After observing the calm and dignified behaviour of the Aborigines and then the hysterical ranting and raving of Mr Tuxworth, I am convinced we have done the right thing.

To all Liberal politicians attempting to dance to the tune orchestrated by the National Party, and who promise to return Ayers Rock to "all Australians", I would hereby like to bestow on you the Royal Order of the Ugly Australian. Hang your heards in shame.

Jan Wall,
Elizabeth Bay Road,
Elizabeth Bay.
October 28

Figure 4.2

In *The Sydney Morning Herald*'s 'Letters to the Editor' page, a group describing themselves as 'Friends of the Redfern Community' respond with disgust to the Northern Territory Government's paid advertisement, 5 November 1985, *The Sydney Morning Herald*, p. 14 [Fairfax]

Figure 4.3

Cartoonist Sean Leahy mocked suggestions that white Australia magnanimously gave 'Ayers Rock' to Indigenous Australians, 28 October 1985, *The Courier-Mail*, p. 4 [Queensland Newspapers Pty Ltd]

> I have never been to Ayers Rock, yet even for me it has become a symbol of Australia – like our present national flag, the Melbourne Cricket Ground or some of our marvellous native birds and animals. I object most strongly to the Government's posturing in handing it over to people who have no better claim to it than I or 15 million other Australians.[18]

News reports evoking the symbolism of 'the Rock' for white Australia reflect shifting historical views about the iconicity of national terrain – those landscape images that help to construct a dominant Australian identity. According to Kay Schaffer in her study of settler-colonial imaginings of place, historically, the bush has been central to self-definition in Australia. But it's a cultural construction that has often excluded 'others' or those outside the mainstream cultural narrative such as women and Indigenous Australians. In the Anglo-Australian tradition, Schaffer writes, there is tension in the appeal of the bush as both a site of heroic exploration and existential threat:

> [the] personification of the bush as the heart, the Interior – [is] a mysterious presence which calls to men for the purposes of exploration and

> discovery but is also a monstrous place in which men may either perish or be absorbed.[19]

The figure of the pioneering bushman informs our understanding of mateship as a 'defining characteristic of the Australian character' since it is in the bonds of mateship that men find solace from the harsh realities of the Australian bush.[20] But as David Carter writes in his analysis of cinematic and televisual depictions of the Australian landscape, the storied myth of the bush in the Australian settler-colonial imagination began to wane in the 1980s in favour of an emptied landscape. In this period, the desert or outback emerged as a source of national identification so that, by the time Carter was writing in the 1990s, it was '... clearly the "red centre" or "wide brown" landscape that now most fully signifies the nation'.[21] In Australian studies scholarship, the Australian desert represents an inverted universe far removed from the civility and rationality of modern urban life where 'things of enigma, privacy, the body, primitive asociality, secrecy, [and] death' dominate.[22] The violence of an infant's disappearance at 'the Rock' in the dead centre of Australia stirred cultural meanings of place and raised questions about settler-colonial belonging in an inhospitable landscape. Nowhere was this more clearly articulated than in the comments of Opposition spokesperson Paul Everingham who, in his objection to the 'Ayers Rock' handover in 1985, told Federal Parliament that 'Non-Aboriginal Australians were being treated only as tourists'.[23]

Among news workers there was support for the historic handover of 'Ayers Rock'. In its coverage of the event, the *Advertiser* reported the significance of 'the Rock' to white Australians was only a recent phenomenon and Aboriginal ties to country ran deep.

> Yet it is only in relatively recent times that this haunting presence in the heart of our continent has begun to occupy a unique place in the national consciousness of white Australians. Less than 50 years ago the few who wanted to see it were being cautioned that the only safe way to get there was by camel. Nowadays, of course, tourists fly in by the plane load. But we are latecomers on the scene. Today, in a ceremony charged with symbolism, the Federal Government will hand over the ownership of Ayers Rock to the Aboriginal people, whose ancestors may have held it sacred thousands of years before the rise of Babylon or Carthage.[24]

In op-eds and letters to the editor, everyday readers applauded the decision to acknowledge Aboriginal land rights. This was no more evident than in reader responses to the Northern Territory Government's full-page paid advertisement in *The Sydney Morning Herald* newspaper opposing the decision. Headlined 'The Rock Belongs to All Australians' (original emphasis, see Figure 4.1) the government declared itself to be 'adamantly opposed' to the transfer of ownership to 'special Australians' who would each derive an annual profit of $75,000 from the leasing arrangement the government brokered. The advertisement generated impassioned responses from readers. One resident of Elizabeth Bay in Sydney wrote to say she was 'convinced we have done the right thing' and to those persuaded by the National Party push to return 'the Rock' to 'all Australians', she said they ought to 'hang their heards in shame [sic]' and bestowed on them the 'Royal Order of the Ugly Australian'.[25] In *The Sydney Morning Herald*'s 'Letters to the Editor' page, a group describing themselves as 'friends of the Redfern Community' responded to the notice with disgust (see Figure 4.2):

> We say: [Prime Minister Bob] Hawke is contributing to the restoration of land to the original owners. Just because white men have divided this country recklessly and sold it to foreign ownership, etc, for 200 years, does not make it morally right … Hawke has not given Australian land away. He has returned Australian

> land to the rightful owners. Congratulations, Mr Hawke, we support you.[26]

The everyday politics of people using pre-digital media to participate in the national conversation about Indigenous sovereignty rehearsed the kind of 'political work' we see in contemporary hashtags on social media.[27] Indeed, the Northern Territory Government's appeal to 'All Australians' opposing the handover of 'Ayers Rock' has a contemporary parallel in the slogans used by #AllLivesMatter protestors, against the #BLM movement.

Tabloid coverage of the 'Ayers Rock' handover ceremony showed elements of sensitivity to the cultural significance of the event for Indigenous Australians. *The Courier-Mail* reported that 'The Aboriginals did not see the occasion as something being returned to them. The massive monolith has always owned them and their ancestors'[28] and proceeded to give voice to traditional owners by quoting a lengthy excerpt from the 'Pitjantjatjara anthem' that featured in the handover ceremony:

> We are many going
> With strength,
> Our brave spirit,
> Others are unable to manage, look after.
> We the holder of many stories,

Forever watch over great country,
Our road today grasped bravely
Is a different story we are learning,
Ears open, understanding.
We speak with happiness,
The country is ours.[29]

The report also featured a cartoon by the artist Leahy, depicting 'Ayers Rock' garlanded with ribbon and two figures running in the foreground, one saying to the other, 'If you spot any cracks – we'll send it back!' Leahy was satirising suggestions that white Australia magnanimously gave 'Ayers Rock' to the Aboriginal people (see Figure 4.3). In the wake of this highly politicised debate in media about Aboriginal land rights and the ownership of 'Ayers Rock', the monolith would again fix the nation's focus for entirely different reasons.

'Ayers Rock' –Azaria Connection

Some three months after the handover ceremony, Azaria's matinee jacket was discovered on 2 February 1986. It was reported to be the latest plot development in a classic 'who-dunit' [sic] set against a foreboding landscape.[30] The search of 'a small area of scrub' at 'the Rock's' base had been postponed because of 'extreme heat' and treacherous conditions:

> The maximum air temperature in the shade was 41C here yesterday. The red earth baked. The heat penetrated relentlessly through the coolest, and the sturdiest, footwear. Tar in the asphalt road which circles the Rock melted. And the heat radiating from the spectacular monolith was remarkable. As one approached the restricted area, 33 metres from the Rock, the temperature increased noticeably. An immediate reaction was to turn around and walk back towards the sticky road.[31]

The inhospitable landscape appeared to repel unwanted guests who, in an effort to avoid the 'unsatisfactory' prospect of a night dig, wielded 'brooms, sieves and lots of patience'.[32] Whether referred to as 'the Rock', 'the base of Ayers Rock', 'near Ayers Rock' or simply 'the site', the location of the matinee jacket figured prominently in news reports of its discovery.[33]

The extract from the *Advertiser* quoted at the outset of this chapter is an example of the way news outlets connected 'Ayers Rock', one of Australia's most recognisable landmarks and its symbolic heart, to the Azaria story. In some cases, the link was uncanny. The day after the ceremony, the *Sunday Territorian* pasted together a front-cover spread of the headlines '"I want truth": Lindy calls for Inquiry' that referred to the Chamberlains' petition for a judicial inquiry into their convictions and 'Chief Jeered at Rock', a report about the Northern Territory Chief Minister, Ian Tuxworth, who was booed at the handover ceremony. Though different stories, Tuxworth features prominently in both when in the opening paragraph of the former article, the *Sunday Territorian* wrote, '"The truth! … that's all I want". This more than anything is what Lindy Chamberlain wants from the Chief Minister, Mr Ian Tuxworth'.[34] The report follows with Lindy issuing her 'strongest public statement to date' about the 'vested Territory interests [of those] who wanted to protect the Yulara investment and tourism at the Rock'.[35] Her comments refer to Tuxworth's predecessor, Paul Everingham, who, after the 1983 announcement by the government to recognise Aboriginal ownership of 'Ayers Rock', expressed concerns that the decision would negatively impact a proposal by the Yulara Interdepartmental Planning team to build a tourism Mecca at 'the Rock'.[36] As *The Sydney Morning Herald* reported in 1983, 'He [Everingham] feared the Commonwealth's decision would jeopardise the future of a $150 million development planned for Ayers Rock' known as the Yulara tourist village.[37] Fears about both the negative publicity generated by dingoes menacing tourists at 'Ayers Rock' and the restrictions on commercial development that might follow the transfer of ownership of the site brought the Azaria story and 'Ayers Rock' handover into sharp focus.

Debates about the 'Ayers Rock' handover also revealed the

commercialisation of the tourist site and Azaria story. Just months before the discovery of the matinee jacket, the Uluru-Kata Tjuta Board of Management fielded strange requests from members of the public hoping to cash in on the 'Ayers Rock' landmark. One film company applied to crash an aeroplane into the soaring rock domes then known as the Olgas (now Kata Tjuta), while another requested boulders be rolled down the side of 'Ayers Rock' as part of a dramatic scene in a spaghetti western.[38] *The Sydney Morning Herald* reported these strange requests in the appropriately headlined story 'Everyone wants a bit of The Rock':

> And the painter Pro Hart once proposed paint-bombing The Rock from the air with water-soluble colours … Other ideas are less ambitious but equally bizarre. Say, setting the world record for a karate kick atop The Rock. Or crushing a piece of the megalith, and selling chips inside plastic cases marked 'This is a piece of The Rock'. The entrepreneur in this case even offered the traditional owners $2 for each chip he sold.[39]

In a satirical poke at the Northern Territory Government for its commercialisation of the sacred site, the article described a typically 'twisted' proposal to stage '… a precision dwarf hurling contest from the top of Ayers Rock. The target?

A matinee jacket pinned to the ground at the base of The Rock'.[40] Although tongue-in-cheek, the reference highlights the symbolic link between public debate about the appropriate use and ownership of 'Ayers Rock' – a symbol of Aboriginal land rights and the site of the sacred handover ceremony – and national conversations about the Chamberlain case.

Key figures in the 'Ayers Rock' handover ceremony also played a pivotal role in Azaria's disappearance and their media representations reveal the intricacies of institutionalised racism in news media of the time. Aboriginal elder Barbara Tjikadu and her husband Nipper Winmatti, who were both expert trackers, are two examples. Tjikadu had followed dingo tracks in the search for Azaria that night and noticed a dusty impression made by the baby's body in the sand hills east of the Chamberlains' tent, presumably when the dingo dropped the infant from its mouth. The elders were also key witnesses at the 1987 Royal Commission of Inquiry into the Chamberlain convictions. In the *Sunday Press Magazine* coverage headlined 'Nipper knows all the tricks', journalist Denis Williams reported, initially mockingly, that Aboriginal trackers remained steadfast in their belief Lindy was innocent: 'Nipper Winamartti [sic]' – the '70-year-old … grizzly tribal elder of the Pitjantjatjara people' 'still' believed that a dingo killed Azaria Chamberlain in August 1980.[41] Williams concocted an elaborate scheme to test the elder's tracking ability by clambering over rocks, sand dunes and scrubland surrounding the 'Ayers Rock' campsite from where Azaria disappeared. For the experiment, Williams changed his shoes several times (even alternating left and right pairs), concealed his shirt in a hole at the rock face, knelt and dragged himself along the ground and, at one stage, wiped away his own tracks. He was later surprised to discover that Nipper could show him the scuff marks and tracks he had made across the sand and even locate the journalist's hidden shirt. It was confirmation for Williams that Nipper was a 'key figure in the [Chamberlain] drama' and 'one of the last masters of the age-old bush craft'[42] whose story about the dingo was to be believed. News reports about key personalities, public figures, symbols and events in the Chamberlain story often threaded the case into the wider fabric of nation at a time when Australia was in the grip of nation-building processes – which historian Manning Clark called 'a quest for identity'.[43] One of those defining events was the Bicentenary of 1988.

'Our oldest story told through ... modern technical and lighting genius'

The year-long celebrations of Australia's Bicentenary marking 200 years since the arrival of British convict ships were in full swing on 26 January 1988. At the official landing site of Port Jackson, tall ships, ferries and row boats of spectators clogged Sydney Harbour, while an estimated 2.5 million people hugged the foreshore. Some descendants of First Fleeters were dressed in period costume, flanked in long stockings, breeches, lace shawls and mop caps in the middle of Australia's sweltering summer.[44] At Lady Macquarie's Chair, protestors gathered at the Aboriginal tent embassy but were soon overrun with spectators keen to secure a view of the harbour festivities.[45] Meanwhile, thousands of Australians took part in two peaceful protest marches, the latter reported by television broadcasters as 'the biggest land rights protest in Australian history' and 'the largest mass demonstration of black solidarity ever staged in Australia'.[46] In the midst of the protests, news coverage of the Bicentenary revealed an official calendar of events aimed at strengthening communal ties between Indigenous and non-Indigenous Australians, as was demonstrated in the Expo 88 extravaganza.

The six-month carnival known as Expo 88 attracted more than 15 million visitors to Brisbane, Queensland, and was the largest event in the bicentennial celebrations. In its coverage of the fair, headlined 'Blacks use Expo to get the other message across',[47] *The Sydney Morning Herald* reported members of Australia's Indigenous community willingly took part in the commemorative events despite vocal protestors in attendance:

> Aborigines have generally been highly critical of

> the Bicentenary and the various events, including Expo, held as part of the 1988 celebrations. Expo's opening by the Queen on April 30 was accorded a large Aboriginal demonstration visible enough to make a considerable impact on visitors and representatives of the 34 exhibiting islands and nations. But not all Aborigines see Expo in that light; for some, it is the perfect forum for educating visitors – Australians and foreigners alike.[48]

By June 1988, it was reported 'two million' Australians had viewed the range of events on offer, demonstrating a 'keen interest in the very essence of the first Australians' spiritual way of life'.[49] One event at the Rainbow Serpent Theatre in Brisbane was aimed at 'modernising' Indigenous history through the dramatic restaging of Dreamtime stories that would illustrate the cultural continuum of Indigenous and settler-colonial history. It was reported to be our oldest story told through a mix of live theatre and clever mystical effects created by modern technical and lighting genius.[50] Knitting Australian Aboriginal and settler-colonial history into a continuous thread of cultural existence projected the image of a cohesive nation at a time when Australia featured prominently on the world stage. The most visual representation of the nation's sudden global platform was the television event 'Australia Live'.

The four-hour television special, 'Australia Live', was the world's biggest ever live telecast and the first commemorative event in the bicentennial calendar, beginning on 1 January 1988. Simulcast by Nine, the ABC and SBS and broadcast on the UK's Channel Four and America's A&E Network, the event was steered by familiar Australian faces in Clive James, Ray Martin and Jana Wendt. The program featured pre-recorded cameos from world leaders such as US President Ronald Reagan and British Prime Minister Margaret Thatcher as well as live crosses to historic landmarks such as 'Ayers Rock', Kakadu and even the remote South Australian town of Kingoonya with its total population of six.[51] It was later acclaimed as a technical feat in Australian broadcasting for reaching regional centres that had never received live transmission. In the event program, modern Australia was described as 'the oldest earth on earth', emphasising less the country's 'timeless past' and more its 'modernity' in the fusion of past and present civilisations through a single historical moment.[52] Arguably, this fiction of continuity was an attempt to project a unified Australian identity while under the gaze of international media.

'What will ordinary citizens learn ... about themselves as a people, as a nation?'

Australia's bicentennial celebrations and presence on the world stage coincided with a significant moment in the Chamberlains' legal battle to clear their names. Three judges of the Northern Territory Supreme Court had been deliberating on the couple's application to have their convictions overturned. On 15 September 1988, the judges unanimously quashed the Chamberlain convictions, after which news headlines shouted 'Lindy innocent',[53] 'Innocent!'[54] and 'Like rising from the dead – Michael'.[55] In news copy a collective sigh of relief greeted the resolution of an affair that began 'on a cold night in August 1980 [and ever since has] ... baffled and divided Australia, been through eight different courts in as many years and cost tens of millions of dollars'.[56]

In the wash up, anxieties shifted to the impact of the Chamberlain saga on Australia's international reputation. *Time* magazine implored: 'But what will ordinary citizens learn from the [Azaria] affair, about themselves as a people, as a nation?'[57] Similarly, *The Courier-Mail* stated that 'an injustice had been done and that all of us in society must bear some responsibility'.[58] It was commonly believed the controversies surrounding the case had been witnessed by 'the world' and the decision in September 1988 to exonerate the couple was another event taking place under the scrutinising gaze of international audiences:

> For the Chamberlains, that decision … meant the culmination of an eight-year battle to make the law, and the world that watched, believe that they did not have anything to do with their daughter's death. Everything that has meant, and the enormous trauma it has entailed, is history. It is now part of a unique and prolonged episode in Australia's system of justice.[59]

As Michael Chamberlain told Alan Jones of Radio 2UE in Sydney, there was an element of 'social guilt' behind the nation's reaction to Azaria's disappearance.[60] It was further compounded by collective guilt over the past and present treatment of Australia's Indigenous population – a struggle that continues today over both settler-colonial legitimacy and Aboriginal land rights. There were concerns that international condemnation would follow news of the couple's exoneration, as it had in response to Australia's treatment of its Indigenous people, which the *Advertiser* recalled:

> Nowadays, [Aboriginal] grievances are known, though imperfectly understood, in many countries beside our own. The presidents of France and of South Africa have seized on them lately, implying for their own rather disreputable

> purposes that Australia is in the process of solving its racial problems by wiping out the Aborigines. The transfer of Ayers Rock may help to offset this slur.[61]

The bicentennial year was also an occasion for the United Nations to formally condemn the abject poverty under which Australia's Aboriginal people were living:

> THE UNITED Nations report declaring that Australian Aborigines are living in 'poverty, misery and extreme frustration' has prompted a knee-jerk response from the Federal Government … Let us be reminded that this is the Bicentenary year. It is the 200th birthday of white European settlement and, therefore, an historic opportunity to reach a civilised (and civilising) compact with the original inhabitants.[62]

The Hawke administration's response to the United Nations report was to allocate further funds to Aboriginal welfare. It was an attempt to address the problems besetting Aboriginal people in the year Australia was 'on show' to the world. According to cultural theorist Deborah Staines, the pattern of injustice marking the 'post-settlement' history of Aboriginal people affected the way in which the nation responded to Azaria's disappearance. The case highlighted a nation refusing to accept, confront and recognise a history of government policies that led to the removal of Aboriginal children and the dispossession of their people and culture:

> [The case] articulated an agenda of coming to terms with the past, reimagining identity, and repositioning Australian values … We need to reconsider the articulation and reception of the Chamberlain case with reference to this historical context, reading it alongside a nation denying its past.[63]

For Staines, the Chamberlain event problematised non-Indigenous relations to the land and the right of white Australia to exercise control over the 'frontier':

> This strange event interrupted a self-serving rhetoric of Australian identity based around notions of settler control of the land, and the dominant white culture's claims to knowledge of that land. The Chamberlains' statements undermined the myth of settler control.[64]

Similar views have been expressed by other scholars writing on the Chamberlain case, such as Noel Sanders and Christine Higgins. Sanders argued that the historical background to the Chamberlain case saw the issue of land ownership culminate in the 'displacement of urban white male society',[65] while Higgins argued the 'cultural opposition' between Indigenous and non-Indigenous Australians was highlighted in the aftermath of Azaria's disappearance.[66] The location of the event provided a battleground for the appropriation of a distinctly 'white' national space. It was a deeply divisive issue along partisan lines as one Catholic clergymen told *The Sydney Morning Herald* in his response to the Coalition's plans to revoke the Aboriginal Land Rights Bill: 'In this Bicentennial year, the year of reconciliation with Aborigines, this racist policy will further the dispossession begun 200 years ago when we first took their land'.[67] Scholarly writings on the Chamberlain case have highlighted the significance of the mystical setting of Azaria's disappearance – the eerie plains of the outback with its contested spaces of belonging and unsettled identities – that shaped cultural meanings of the event.[68] By 1988, it was clear the dingo baby story would be irrevocably tied to the wider story of nation, and two cultural productions – a film and a museum collection – would confirm this fact.

Evil Angels and an Eternity Collection

The day after the Chamberlain convictions were quashed, the Adelaide *Advertiser* rightly predicted the upcoming release of the film *Evil Angels* was a signal Azaria's story was moving 'into wider realms of mythology'.[69] Director Fred Schepisi's film *Evil Angels* (*A Cry in the Dark*) was released in cinemas around the country on 3 November 1988. The production was part of the new phase of cinematic nationalism in which the Australian Government implemented a range of initiatives to promote the arts. Led by Prime Minister Gough Whitlam, the aim was to '... develop a national identity through artistic expression and to project Australia's image in other countries by means of the arts'.[70] There were a number of scenes within the film that captured an 'authentic' sweeping outback landscape that has historically symbolised the national character, its values and sentiments.[71] As in the earlier Australian feature *Picnic at Hanging Rock* (1975), the natural landscape in *Evil Angels* was animated through point-of-view and high angle shots that miniaturised characters on screen and pitted them against a mysterious, inscrutable force. *Picnic at Hanging Rock* (1975) was a milestone Australian film for its projection of non-Indigenous Australia's artful relation to the bush in new and sophisticated ways, signalling a turning point in the style and tastes of local productions. Released at the end of this new wave of Australian cinema, *Evil Angels* is an example of filmic preoccupations with the Australian landscape at the time.

Producers of *Evil Angels* cast American actor Meryl Streep in the lead role of Lindy Chamberlain. They were likely inspired by the success of the blockbuster *Crocodile Dundee* (1986), which re-played the Australian legend in ways that were self-referential and pitched at American audiences. Streep's appointment was strategic given the pressures of film financing and an increase in local production costs in the 1980s that caused filmmakers to rely on the billing of well-known actors to gain international publicity and promotion.[72] The nationality of the Hollywood legend was a topic of concern amongst critics who questioned her ability to authentically portray an Australian middle-class Christian woman. As *Time* magazine asked: 'Can Meryl Streep simulate a truly convincing nasal Strine whine? Is Robert Redford really handsome enough? Why not Paul Hogan?'[73] While *The New York Times* had touted Robert Redford to play the dashing Michael Chamberlain,[74] New Zealand actor Sam Neill nabbed the role. For some it was recognition of Neill's honorary Australian status after appearing in several successful local productions including *My Brilliant Career* (1979). Films of the period were 'applauded for their Australianness',[75] a fact that was reflected in gross ticket sales for *Evil Angels* that topped $6.908 million at the US Box Office,[76] and in the film's release across Scandinavian and

European markets including an honorary screening in 1991 at the Centre Georges Pompidou in Paris.

As well as the memorialisation of the dingo baby story in a Hollywood film, in 1988 the National Museum of Australia curated a series of Azaria Chamberlain artefacts for its 'Eternity' exhibit. Within the permanent collection are Azaria's black dress with matching panties and red knitted booties (an outfit that inspired many conspiracy theories), the wooden coffin used as a prop in Michael's antismoking classes that aroused suspicion because of its child-like size, and a section of dashboard from the Chamberlains' Holden Torana car that the trial prosecution team alleged had been sprayed with Azaria's blood after Lindy slit her throat with a pair of scissors. Forensic investigations would later reveal the apparent presence of 'arterial foetal blood spray' was in fact the overspray of a sound deadening agent applied during the car's manufacturing process. Today, the museum houses more than 350 objects donated by or purchased from the Chamberlain family and an additional 200 items from other sources connected to the case.

Given efforts to promote an Australian national identity in Australia's bicentennial year, the curation of the Azaria exhibit was significant; so too was its proximity to another important spectacle marking the story of first contact and Australia's growth as a nation. Known as the Bicentenary travelling exhibition, the hand-picked assortment boasted 'Captain

Cook's telescope, armour from the Kelly gang, Dame Nellie Melba's tiara, an Aboriginal breastplate, a stump-jump plough and a dingo trap'.[77] While commemorating different occasions, the exhibitions were linked by the timing of their public display in a period of Australian national mythologisation. The artefacts themselves resemble what Susan M Pearce calls 'message-bearing entit[ies]' because they encase the attitudes, beliefs and cultures of the historical periods in which they were wrought.[78] As time travelling objects, they freeze-frame the past in a continuing present and are rendered powerful by a 'real' relationship to the events they recollect and the 'impulse' that created them.[79] In both collections, the National Museum assembled objects of national significance that purported to symbolise who we are as a nation – objects that were first put on show in 1988 for the Australian public and the wider world to see. The decision to memorialise the Chamberlain case in the national gallery situated in the country's capital, firmly fixed the event in Australia's collective memory. For celebrated Australian author Thomas Keneally, the Chamberlain case collides with other moments of national significance:

> Remember the day: Political Commentator Laurie Oakes made a small claim to journalistic immortality by revealing the contents of John Howard's third budget two days early; the 50th

> anniversary of the linking of the Harbour Bridge span had Sydney's press in nostalgic mood; Ian Sinclair was preparing to be reinstated to the Fraser ministry after being found not guilty four days before of nine charges including forging and uttering; a 10-ounce middy of beer cost 52c; and at Ayers Rock in Central Australia, nine-week-old Azaria Chamberlain disappeared from her family's holiday tent.[80]

In the company of other memorable markers in the nation's past, the Azaria saga was often read and understood through coincident moments such as the symbolic 'Ayers Rock' handover ceremony and bicentennial commemorations. The 'symbols of Australian-ness' the Chamberlain case evoked – considered here in 'Ayers Rock', the dingo and Indigenous Australians – interlocked the Azaria story in a chain of political, social and cultural signifiers that constitute important sites of memory in the history of the country. Media coverage of the case provided a vehicle for discussion about nationhood, race and identity in the 1980s – a debate that continues to this day and often pivots on the slogan 'Sorry, not sorry'.

CONCLUSION

> Definitely not trial by media. I'll say that from the rooftop, because ... there was no need to be. It was all there ... with no need of an adjective even, let alone, beating the story up.[1]

'A dingo's got my baby. Five words that will forever divide the nation'. That was the promo for Channel 7's documentary broadcast on the eve of the 40th anniversary of Azaria's disappearance. Dubbed 'The Lindy Tapes', the TV special was the result of a six-month investigation by the 7News *Spotlight* team that unearthed 80 hours of secret tape recordings of police officers weaving an elaborate plot to frame Lindy for her daughter's murder. For industry pundits, installing journalist Denham Hitchcock as the host was a notable irony. For it was his father, famed TV newsman Kevin Hitchcock, who 36 years earlier hosted the documentary 'Azaria: A Question of Evidence' (1984) that made startling claims about the Chamberlain convictions and became a key piece of evidence used by Chamberlain support groups to agitate for Lindy's release (see Chapter 2). The Channel 7 news documentary was yet another instance of a news-led investigation into the Chamberlain convictions – now 40 years after the event – trumpeting the grave miscarriage of justice that had taken place.

Historically, the media have been an easy target to blame for the Chamberlain miscarriage of justice. In the 1980s, a feminist scholarly push for 'the media [to] be put on trial for murder' led to scathing criticism of the fourth estate in Australia.[2] The reason was that the guilty verdict handed-down at the Supreme Court in 1982 was a 'media-contaminated conclusion'[3] supported by 'thousands of Australians who aided and abetted' the process.[4] Ordinary members of the public were swayed by the 'media's lust to kill a defendant's right to be presumed innocent'[5] and its 'perception of Lindy Chamberlain as a dangerous woman'.[6] Ultimately, it was the 'Australian dingo press'[7] that thwarted any hope of a fair trial for the Chamberlains.

In 1990, the case against the media was dramatized into a play first performed at La Trobe and Monash Universities and later at the Athenaeum Theatre in Melbourne. The defendant (the media) stood before a court, '… charged with killing Lindy Chamberlain's chance of a fair trial'.[8] Expert witnesses were called in this mock scenario, among them leading feminist scholars Dianne Johnson, Kerryn Goldsworthy and Catherine Rogers, whose dialogue was taken from their own public statements about media culpability. The media were represented by four journalists (two men and two women) whose scripts were excerpts from press reports of the time. At its public performance, the play was proclaimed '... a dramatization of the persecution and the trial by media of a woman denied the right said to be fundamental to the Australian criminal justice system – the right to be presumed innocent until proven guilty in a court of law'.[9]

By the turn of the millennium, opinion about the media's role in the Chamberlain saga had varied little. In her collection of essays on the Chamberlain case *Lindy Chamberlain revisited: A 25th anniversary retrospective* (2005), Adrian Howe argued the infant's tragic death was transformed by 'almost every media outlet, but especially the press, into a ridiculous and savage tale', in which 'fictions of fantasy' were produced.[10] But the 25th anniversary was an occasion to revisit generalisations about the way everyday Australians responded to the dingo baby story. Howe's ground-breaking study of the Chamberlain Papers, containing 20,000 letters and cards written mostly to Lindy, painted the portrait of a 'kinder, gentler public' who were 'on the Chamberlains' side'. Until recently, it's been a commonplace to point a wagging finger at the Australian public for the persecution the Chamberlains suffered. A Gallup poll in 1984 showed 76.8 per cent of Australians believed Lindy Chamberlain was guilty of murder.[11] Talkback radio was clogged with callers spitting about mothers murdering babies, Lindy's cold look, Michael's posturing and the unlikelihood of a dingo culprit. But the archives prove public support existed and researchers have urged us to celebrate those impervious to the 'media-driven hysteria'.[12] Unlike the smaller number of 'nut jobs' and 'nasties' who also wrote to Lindy and whose 'narrow, misogynous and media contaminated viewpoints have been fully canvassed elsewhere, in the media itself, in dingo jokes and in various published analyses of the case', those who wrote in support of Lindy were apparently immune from the hype, the headlines and the publicity.[13] Howe's important research provided a new historical interpretation of the role of the Australian public in the long-running saga. Yet, the Chamberlain story has always been one of media savagery.

The second decade of the 'Noughties' was another moment in which to reflect on the predations of the Australian media when the case was again in the headlines during the fourth and final Coronial Inquest into Azaria's disappearance. That inquest had, once and for all, found a dingo responsible for the infant's death. In its coverage of the inquest, the ABC's Correspondents Report considered the lessons of the dingo baby saga for Australia:

> … [what] might be learned from the Chamberlains' 32-year battle for the truth: that people – and most definitely the media – should not rush to judge others as guilty, just because they don't meet some preconceived ideal of an innocent, grieving parent, or because their story seems too fantastic.[14]

News outlets rushed to judge Lindy guilty. Journalists instigated the witch hunt. Everyday Australians were duped by 'fake news'. Malicious gossip found its way into the tabloids and leading print dailies. The media 'converged on the Chamberlains like a hungry pack'.[15] These kinds of claims have stood for decades, mostly uncontested, in scholarly, media and public opinion about the case and who or what is to bear responsibility for the greatest miscarriage of justice the nation has ever seen.

There is no doubting the Chamberlains were hounded by the press, tracked by news helicopters, tailgated by journalists, jostled in media scrums, illegally snapped by the 'paps' and had their private conversations secretly recorded. No Australian family before or since has been subjected to such prolonged media attention and scrutiny over 40 years. But the claim an 'Australian dingo press' thwarted the chance of a fair trial for the Chamberlains is based on the existence of a wholly prejudicial media. Not only does this entrenched view overlook the diversity of news coverage of the case but also the seam of journalists whose investigations challenged the guilty verdict and played a critical role in the pro-Chamberlain movement, notably Malcolm Brown (*Sydney Morning Herald*), Kevin Childs (*The Age*), Kevin Hitchcock (Channel Ten), Mike Lester (Channel Nine), Ken Blanch (*Courier-Mail*), Bill Hitchings (*Herald*) and Jim Oram (*Daily Telegraph*). Frank Alcorta from *The Northern Territory News* deserves to be singled out for issuing an ultimatum to the Northern Territory Government that forced Lindy's release from prison in 1986. As the *Azaria Newsletter* and activist pamphlets reveal, favourable news reports galvanised Chamberlain support groups and were instrumental in the judicial inquiry into the Chamberlain convictions (see Chapter 2).

Herald journalist, Bill Hitchings, offers a fascinating insight into news media reporting of the Chamberlain case. When I asked him in an interview whether he'd ever been pressured to adopt a particular angle on the story, he exclaimed, 'I've never been censored by anyone, least of all by Rupert Murdoch, believe it or not'. It was not the persuasions of a newspaper proprietor that Hitchings believes sealed Lindy's fate but, rather, failed science and the law:

> … the evidence was of course that she'd done

> it. And the evidence was very powerful … you had the world's leading forensic scientist, a fellow called James Cameron who had worked on the shroud of Turin, and various other things, he was considered, you know, 'THE man', and of course, everyone was almost in awe of him, certainly the jury was, and he said she did it.[16]

Hitchings firmly argues the Crown case against the Chamberlains was so shocking there was no need for garnish:

> The case was that this young handsome mother, this daughter of a church pastor, the wife of a handsome young man, with this beautiful child, killed her baby in the wilderness, at Ayers Rock, by cutting its throat, to the point where it decapitated the child's head. That in itself, those were facts, or at least facts as they were put. Now you don't need any beating up or trial by media, to garnish that story, it's there. So trial by media was just a myth.[17]

Though a myth for some, the trial by media thesis has dominated critical discussion of the Chamberlain case and is mostly uncontested. I say 'mostly' because Australian literary treasure Frank Moorhouse AM was one radical dissenter in the intellectual ranks. Moorhouse argued that the predisposition amongst intellectuals to view the media as 'a tight collective agency in the society representing or promoting or giving privileged voice to specific interests … [is] without a researched basis'.[18] Indeed, the media is no more unanimous in opinion than the multiple publics that are constituted by it. Often we talk of the media as a homologous institution: an unruly rat bag responsible for a range of social and psychological ills such as narcissism, loneliness, negative body image, mass shootings, teen suicides, gaming addictions and even viral outbreaks and global pandemics. However, when we 'tut-tut' in whispered tones, shake our heads in disbelief, and wring our hands in collective outrage at 'the media', we push responsibility away from others – governments, institutions, corporates and structures. We distance ourselves from 'the problem' and demand the media-makers be held to account, forgetting that the media-makers are among us and that our lives are lived in media, rather than beside it.[19] This is to say that journalists do not admit or exclude a given reality 'out there',[20] as if an objective state existed beyond media influence. As Catharine Lumby writes:

> The contemporary media doesn't simply report on events – it helps produce them. The intensive nature of media coverage makes it difficult for

> anyone to claim that it's possible to clearly separate high-profile events from their representation in the media. It follows then that it's also impossible to judge media coverage solely by the veracity or objectivity with which it represents an event. It's not only that the distance between the media and real events has all but disappeared, but that the illusion of a unified viewing point has vanished with it.[21]

Since we (in western democracies at least) cannot stand outside the media-reality loop and live in a world without media, it is us who comprise those mediated publics. So it follows, just like the society whose views it claims to represent, the media is a platform for varied and diverse perspectives and any analysis of its function or, indeed, responsibility, must recognise this fact.

Rather than a 'trial by media', the Chamberlain case more closely resembles a 'media event' that was relayed live to intimate audiences and is now inseparable from the representations it has inspired over 40 years. As detailed in Chapter 1, the Chamberlain case coincided with rapid advancements in communications and satellite technology and the increasing commercialisation of media that profoundly changed the style, content and delivery of news. The 1980s saw so-called tabloid practices leech into the broadsheet press – as we've seen in the carving of characters like the dingo, the mother and 'Ayers Rock' in Chamberlain news reports. In the same period, tabloid TV was also celebrating its heyday in a shift towards entertaining stories, formats and spectacles.

Early coverage of Azaria's disappearance also coincided with a widening of the sphere of public debate that more closely resembles the participatory and interactive digital media we recognise today: a virtual tower of Babel with its collision of tongues, cacophony of voices and diverse perspectives. In the 1980s, ordinary Australians used letters, pamphlets and circulars to participate in a case that had divided the nation (see Chapter 2). Some interventions, such as those preserved in the National Library of Australia's Chamberlain Papers and catalogued under 'nut', 'nasty' and 'unusual', rehearsed the trollish behaviours that are so ubiquitous on social media today. Others, who wrote heartfelt letters of support to Lindy or coordinated their protest efforts through newsletters, pamphlets and other petitions now archived in the State Library of New South Wales, comprise mediatised counter-publics. Those counter-publics used both traditional and emerging media technologies as a public platform for the dissemination of their views about the Chamberlains, in interventions no less significant than the splashing of our political opinions on social media today.

We can also read late 20th century changes to the production of celebrity in news coverage of the Chamberlains, particularly Lindy (see Chapter 3). When her daughter disappeared on 17 August 1980, Lindy was an 'ordinary' woman living in the remote Queensland mining town of Mt Isa. By the end of the decade, however, there could 'only be one candidate for the title *face of the 80s* in Australia – Lindy Chamberlain'.[22] As I've shown in Chapter 3, Lindy's behaviour, mode of dress and shifting physical shape brought about by pregnancy, weight loss and, more recently a thyroid condition, were meticulously detailed in media reports. Her celebrity transition coincided with the elevation of 'ordinary' individuals, the widening of cultural fields from which celebrities, traditionally, have been plucked, and the development of a modern public relations industry promoting public figures. In the midst of the unrelenting scrutiny of Lindy's appearance, there were times when she sought to control, self-manage and shape her own image. By modifying aspects of her dress, behaviour and public performance and employing the services of a press agent to negotiate her fee-paying appearances, Lindy began to exercise greater control over her public self.

Taking charge of her own narrative is one of the reasons for Lindy's emergence as the human face of wrongful persecution and the benchmark of injustice in Australia. When British tourist Joanne Lees was wrongly accused in July 2001 of murdering her boyfriend, Peter Falconio, in the Australian outback, *New Idea* magazine declared the case to have 'Echoes of Azaria' in 'A cry in the dark, a woman under suspicion and a loved one dead in the desert'.[23] Three years later, the same magazine reported that the 'harrowing images of media scrums and the outpouring of emotion' typifying Lindy Chamberlain's 'ordeal' now surrounded another woman, Schapelle Corby, who had maintained her innocence despite allegations of drug smuggling into Bali.[24] As the women's glossy illustrated, Lindy not only stands as a figure of persecution and an authority on injustice, but as a media elder stateswoman and expert source.

Key cultural and social developments during a period of national mythologising also impacted the way the Chamberlain story was read in the 1980s. As I argued in Chapter 4, the Hawke Government's decision to return 'Ayers Rock' to its traditional owners in 1985 revived settler-colonial anxieties about the land and non-Indigenous relations to it. The infant's disappearance occurred in a much contested ideological terrain – an ancient sacred site for Indigenous Australians and the symbolic 'red heart' of white Australia.[25] It was in the shadow of the monolith that the famous matinee jacket was discovered, too, just months after the official handover ceremony. Then, in 1988, the Supreme Court of Darwin quashed the couple's convictions and a Hollywood film about the case was released to local and international audiences along with a collection of Chamberlain artefacts permanently installed in the National Museum of Australia. Concerns about the impact of the Chamberlain injustice on Australia's international reputation tapped into the bicentennial commemorations of a country eager to overcome racial tensions while in the midst of colonising processes. By virtue of its proximity to events and the meanings with which they were imbued, the Azaria story became symbolically tied to the national story and entwined in debates about nationhood, identity and belonging at this time.

It's a narrative that resists closure – a 'never-ending story'[26] about a woman who touched the 'Australian psyche' and, as such, this book neither claims to be nor will be the final word on the role of the news media in the Chamberlain case. To date there have been 17 books (including this one) published on the Azaria saga, a Hollywood film, an opera, a TV mini-series, podcasts, a weight of theatre productions, television and radio broadcasts and documentaries, as well as academic papers, PhD and masters theses and countless newspaper and magazine articles. Our cultural history is awash with allusions to the Chamberlain story, often in unlikely contexts. In 2002, Australian Internet service provider, OzEmail, splashed a bold, full-page advertisement in *The Sun-Herald* declaring 'The Dingo Did It' (Figure 5.1). The fine print read, 'If you're angry about DingoBlue going out backwards, we don't blame you. But don't be left high and dry. Come over to an Internet Service Provider you can rely on'. The ad was an attempt to persuade customers of rival Internet provider DingoBlue, which had recently gone into receivership, to switch to a more reliable service in OzEmail. And yet, the Australian legal system's ruling that the dingo had in fact 'done it' was only officially confirmed in June 2012 at the fourth and final inquest when Coroner Elizabeth Morris apologised unreservedly to the Chamberlain family for the loss of their 'special and loved daughter and sister'.

A panoply of views informed news coverage of the Chamberlain case. Some reports were sensationalised, others less so, and others still defied the gospel of public opinion polls chorusing the Chamberlains' guilt. *Herald* heavyweight Malcolm Brown was one of those courageous reporters whose decades-long coverage was instrumental to the pro-Chamberlain movement. While there were feral elements in the worst tabloid instincts and sometimes deplorable newsgathering tactics exercised in pursuit of the Azaria story, the news media were also central to the Free Lindy campaign and the quashing of the Chamberlain convictions. Even today, media-led investigations continue to unearth new evidence corroborating the Chamberlains' story of a dingo abduction and exposing the campaign to frame Lindy for her daughter's murder, as the recent Channel 7 news special demonstrates.

Overall, my intention here has been to illustrate how the Chamberlain case has set an example for the way modern media events develop, having coincided with the expanding role of the media as the chief vehicle of the public sphere and an elemental part of modern life. Rather than a 'feral media' – a rabid institution privileging only dominant interests – the media resembled a shifting arena of public contest and debate. There was no resounding chant among news outlets. We cannot speak of 'the media' any more than we can speak of 'the public' as a harmonious assembly. What the Chamberlains have endured is not so much a savage media, but a savage injustice.

March 10, 2002 THE SUN-HERALD

THE DINGO DID IT

If you're angry about dingo blue going out backwards, we don't blame you. But don't be left high and dry. Come over to an Internet Service Provider you can rely on. OzEmail. If you join our OzEunlimited $24.95* plan today and you're a Dingo Blue customer, not only will you get our acclaimed 24x7 technical support, but we'll also give you the **FIRST THREE MONTHS FREE***. So don't make the same mistake twice by going back to an ISP that may not be here for the long haul. Call 132 884 now or visit www.ozemail.com.au.

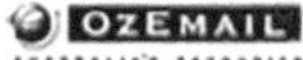

Figure 5.1

An advertisement in *The Sun-Herald* for Australian Internet Service Provider, OzEmail appealing to customers of rival, DingoBlue, to switch to a more reliable service, 10 March 2002, *The Sun-Herald*, p. 30 [Fairfax]

NOTES

Introduction

1 The de-identified tweets reproduced here were posted with one or more of the following hashtags on 9 August 2010, 10 January 2017 and 2 August 2018: #thedingotookmybaby #dingobaby #LindyChamberlain #MichaelChamberlain #Azaria and #Australiantruecrime

2 Chamberlain-Creighton, L. (n.d.) *Why did this happen?* lindychamberlain.com

https://lindychamberlain.com/the-story/why-did-this-happen/

3 For more Australian folkloric responses to the Chamberlain case see Seal, G. (1987). Azaria Chamberlain and the Media Charivari. *Australian Folklore, 1*(March), 68–95.

4 Valentine, A. (2017). *Letters to Lindy: A Mother's Loss, A Nation's Obsession*. Currency Press pp. 38–45.

5 Howe, A. (2005). *Lindy Chamberlain 'revisited': A 25th Anniversary Retrospective.* Southwood Press p. 60, p. 37.

6 Howe (2005) p. 12.

7 Marcus J (1989). Prisoner of Discourse: The Dingo, the Dog and the Baby. In A. Howe (Ed.). *Lindy Chamberlain 'revisited': A 25th Anniversary Retrospective.* (p. 202). Southwood Press.

8 Chamberlain, M. & Tarling, L. (1999). *Beyond Azaria: Black Light, White Light.* Information Australia p. xiv.

9 Howe (2005) p. 2.

10 Craik, J. (2009). The Azaria Chamberlain Case: Blind Spot or Black

Hole in Australian Cultural Memory. In D. Staines, M. Arrow, & K. Biber. *The Chamberlain Case: Nation, Law, Memory*. (p.272). Australian Scholarly Publishing.

11 Bruce-Smith, A. (2020, January 29). Porn, Mass Surveillance and a Certain Dingo/Baby story lead stellar 2020 FODI line-up. *Pedestrian TV.* https://www.pedestrian.tv/news/festival-of-dangerous-ideas-2020/.

12 McKay, B. & Middleweek, B. (2012, June 8). The Media and Lindy Chamberlain and Reporting Criminal Matters in the Northern Territory Today. *ABC Media Report*. https://www.abc.net.au/radionational/programs/archived/ mediareport/the-media-and-lindy-chamberlain2c-and-reporting- criminal-matte/4064942

13 Chamberlain, L. (1990). *Through My Eyes: An Autobiography.* William Heinemann p. 760.

14 Moorhouse, F. (1993). The Azaria Chamberlain Case (1980–86): Hysteria and the Intellectuals. *Australian Cultural History, 12*, 160–75.

15 Martin, R. (1986, March 2). Chamberlain interview with Ray Martin. *60 Minutes*. Nine Network.

16 *Sun-Herald*, 19 September 1982.

17 Dayan, D. & Katz, E. (1992). *Media Events: The Live Broadcasting of History.* Harvard University Press p. 5.

18 Wark, M. (1994). *Virtual Geography: Living with Global Media Events*. Indiana University Press p. vii.

19 For an example of the continuation of media events in a 21st century Chinese context see Wanning, S. (2014). Media Events: Past, Present and Future. *Sociology Compass, 8*(5), 461.

20 I have chosen to refer to the site of Azaria's disappearance as 'Ayers Rock' or 'the Rock' rather than 'Uluru', the name given by the Yankunytjatjara and Pitjantjatjara people that we use today, to capture the colourful and controversial debates about ownership of the site that intersected with the dingo baby story in the 1980s. Throughout the book, I have placed inverted commas around these terms to highlight their contestable nature.

21 Howe (2005) p. 14

22 For further information about the emergence of 'self-presentational media' or social media that enables individuals to self-present and self-promote see Marshall, P.D. (2010). The promotion and presentation of the self: celebrity as marker of presentational media. *Celebrity Studies, 1*(1), 35–48. http://doi:10.1080/19392390903519057

23 Cunningham, A. (1997). Icons, Symbolism and Recordkeeping: The Lindy Chamberlain and Eddie Mabo Papers in the National Library of Australia. *Australian Academic and Research Libraries*, 28(2), 103.

Chapter 1: Media Before Megxit

1 *Sun-Herald*, 26 September 1982.

2 Graham, B. (2020, January 10). Australia's brutal reaction to royal saga. *The Daily Examiner*. https://www.dailyexaminer.com.au/news/australias-brutal-reaction- to-royal-saga/3918273/

3 On the impacts of women's visibility in digital culture see Yelin, H. & Clancy, L. (2020). Doing impact work while female: Hate tweets, 'hot potatoes' and having 'enough of experts.' *European Journal of Women's Studies*, March, 4. doi:10.1177/1350506820910194

4 Ross, M. (2020, January 20). Harry and Meghan: Do the disturbing origins of 'Megxit' mean we should stop using it? *Mercury News*. https://www.mercurynews.com/2020/01/20/harry-and-meghan- the-disturbing-origins-of-megxit-mean-it-should-go-away/

5 Yelin and Clancy (2020).

6 *The Sun*, 18 August 1980.

7 *Daily Mirror*, 18 August 1980.

8 *The Australian*, 19 August 1980.

9 *Courier-Mail*, 19 August 1980.

10 Middleweek, B. & McKay, B. (2012, March 26). Interview with B

Hitchings via phone.

11 Boukes, M., Jones, N.P. & Vliegenthart, R. (2020). Newsworthiness and story prominence: How the presence of news factors relates to upfront position and length of news stories. *Journalism*

https://doi. org/10.1177/1464884919899313

12 Johansson, S. (2007). *Reading tabloids: Tabloid Newspapers and their Readers.* Södertörns högskola p. 7.

13 Bird, S.E. (2009). Tabloidization: What is it, and does it really matter? In Zelizer, B. *The Changing Faces of Journalism: Tabloidization, Technology, and Truthiness* (p. 40). Routledge. DOI: 10.13140/2.1.2223.0404

14 Macdonald, G. (1980). *One hundred years: Wellcome: in pursuit of excellence.* The Wellcome Foundation Limited p. 12

https://wellcomelibrary.org/item/ b20457315#?c=0&m=0&s=0&cv=13&z=-0.0731%2C0.1637%2C1 .398%2C0.7073

15 Macdonald (1980) p. 12.

16 Macdonald (1980) p. 25.

17 Bird in Zelizer (2009).

18 Serazio, M. (2009). Rethinking a Villain, Redeeming a Format: The Crisis and Cure in Tabloidization. In Zelizer, B. *The Changing Faces of Journalism: Tabloidization, Technology, and Truthiness* (p. 14). Routledge. DOI: 10.13140/2.1.2223.0404

19 Bird in Zelizer (2009).

20 Mayer, H. (1964). *The Press in Australia.* Lansdowne, p. 21.

21 Bird in Zelizer (2009).

22 Gossel, D. (2017, February 23). Tabloid Journalism. *Encyclopedia Britannica.* https://www.britannica.com/topic/tabloid-journalism

23 Lumby, C. (1999). *Gotcha: Life in a Tabloid World.* Allen & Unwin p. xii.

24 Lumby (1999) p. xii.

25 Lumby (1999) pp. xii–xiii.

26 Balme, J. & O'Connor, S. (2016). Dingoes and Aboriginal social organization in Holocene Australia. *Journal of Archaeological Science: Reports*, 7, 775–81.

27 Rose, D.B. (2002, September 7). *The Dead, the Missing, the Lost, and the Voiceless: Some Thoughts on Extinction from a Dingo Perspective* [Conference presentation] Ninth Conference on Hunting & Gathering (CHAGS), Edinburgh. www.abdn.ac.uk/chags9/1-rose.htm

28 Balme & O'Connor (2016) p. 777.

29 Parker, M.A. (2006). *Dingoes and Aboriginal social organization in Holocene Australia* [PhD thesis, University of Tasmania] https://eprints.utas.edu.au/1196/2/02Whole.pdf

30 *Illawarra Mercury*, 19 August 1980.

31 *Central Western Daily*, 19 August 1980.

32 *Daily Mirror*, 18 August 1980.

33 Wilson, B. (1990). *The Making of a Modern Myth: The Chamberlain Case and the Australian Media*. [unpublished MA Thesis] Murdoch University p. 64.

34 Sanders, N. (1993). Azaria Chamberlain and popular culture. In Frow, J. & Morris, M. (Eds.), *Australian Cultural Studies: A Reader*. Allen & Unwin p. 97.

35 Sanders, N in Frow & Morris (1995) p. 178.

36 *Daily Telegraph*, 19 August 1980.

37 *Daily Mirror*, 18 August 1980.

38 *The Age*, 3 February 1982.

39 Bryson J (1988). *Evil Angels*. Penguin Books p. 394.

40 *Daily Telegraph*, 19 August 1980.

41 Skovsgaard, M. (2014). A tabloid mind? Professional values and organizational pressures as explanations of tabloid journalism. *Media, Culture & Society, 36*(2): 200–18.

42 *The Advertiser*, 19 August 1980.

43 For examples see *The Australian*, 21 August 1980; *Daily Telegraph*, 20 August 1980.

44 *The Age*, 20 August 1980; *Daily Mirror*, 19 August 1980.

45 *Sydney Morning Herald*, 19 August 1980.

46 *The Sun*, 18 August 1980.

47 *Daily Mirror*, 7 and 15 October 1980; *The Sun*, 23 October.

48 *The Sun*, 4 September 1980.

49 *The Sun*, 4 September 1980.

50 Shears, R. (1982). *Azaria: The Mysterious Disappearance of Azaria Chamberlain*. Sphere Books p. 1; Bryson (1988) p. 28; Grace, H (2005). A Shroud of Evidence. In A. Howe (Ed.), *Lindy Chamberlain 'revisited': A 25th Anniversary Retrospective*. Southwood Press p. 192.

51 *Central Western Daily*, 19 August 1980.

52 *Courier-Mail*, 19 August 1980.

53 *Observer*, London, 5 September 1982.

54 *The Age*, 19 August 1980.

55 *Sun-Herald*, 19 September 1982.

56 *The Age*, 1 February 1982.

57 *Daily Telegraph*, 4 November 1982.

58 *The Sun*, 18 August 1980.

59 *The Sun*, 4 September 1980.

60 *Sun-Herald*, 22 February 1981.

61 Michael was a keen photographer and the couple had been advised to wait at the campsite and not join the search party in case there was news, see Chamberlain (1990).

62 *Sun-Herald*, 22 February 1981.

63 *Daily Telegraph*, 1 November 1982.

64 *Daily Telegraph*, 1 November 1982.

65 *Daily Telegraph*, 1 November 1982.

66 *Sun-Herald*, 26 September 1982.

67 *Sun-Herald*, 26 September 1982.

68 Windschuttle, K. (1984). *The Media: A New Analysis of the Press: Television, Radio and Advertising*. Penguin Books p. 38.

69 Windschuttle (1984) p. 38.

70 *Sydney Morning Herald*, 20 February 1981.

71 Sanders in Frow & Morris (1993) p. 88.

72 Bryson (1988) p. 232.

73 *Sydney Morning Herald*, 20 February 1981.

74 *Sydney Morning Herald*, 20 February 1981.

75 *Sydney Morning Herald*, 20 February 1981.

76 Bowcott, O. (2020). Judges' sentencing in high-profile court cases to be televised, *The Guardian*, 16 January. https://www.theguardian.com/law/2020/jan/16/judges-sentencing-in-high-profile-court-cases-to-be-televised

77 Scannell, P. (1996). *Radio, Television and Modern Life*. Blackwell p. 84.

78 Sun, W. (2014). Media Events: Past, Present and Future. *Sociology Compass, 8*(5), 457–467.

79 *Sydney Morning Herald*, 21 February 1981.

80 *Sun-Herald*, 31 October 1982.

81 Sunday Extra, *The Age*, 10 September 1983.

82 Windschuttle (1984) pp. 39–40.

83 Windschuttle (1984) p. 31.

84 *Daily Mirror*, 24 November 1981.

85 Turner, G. (2005). *Ending the affair: the decline of television current affairs in Australia*. University of New South Wales p. 52.

86 Brown, J. (1982). *Eyewitness News*. Channel 10 [Courtesy of the National Film and Sound Archive].

87 Anderson, B. (1991). *Imagined Communities: Reflections on the origin and spread of nationalism*. Verso.

88 Turner (2005) p. 50.

89 For an example of the argument soft news leads to the 'dumbing down' of society see Nguyen, A. (2012). The Effect of Soft News on Public Attachment to the News. *Journalism Studies*, 13(5–6), 706–717. DOI:10.1080/1461670X.2012.664318

90 Steiner, L. (2005). The 'gender matters' debate in journalism: Lessons from the front. In Allan, S. (Ed.), *Journalism: Critical Issues*. Open University Press, 42.

91 Mayes, T. (2000). Submerging in 'Therapy News'. *British Journalism Review, 11*(4), 35.

92 Van Zoonen, L. (1998). One of the Girls? The Changing Gender of Journalism. In C. Carter, G. Branston & S. Allan (Eds.), *News, Gender and Power,* Routledge p. 36; see also Chambers, D., Steiner, L. & Fleming, C. (2004). *Women and Journalism*. Routledge.

93 Bird, S.E. (2000). Audience demands in a murderous market: Tabloidization in US television news. In C. Sparks, & J. Tulloch (Eds.), *Tabloid Tales: Global Debates Over Media Standards*. Roman & Littlefield Publishers p. 219; see also Lumby (1999).

94 Bird (2000).

Chapter 2: Trolling Before Twitter

1 Seal, G. (1987). Azaria Chamberlain and the Media Charivari, *Australian Folklore*, 1 (March), 71.

2 Seal (1987).

3 Seal, G. (2009). Dread, Delusion and Globalisation: From Azaria to Schapelle. In D. Staines, M. Arrow & K. Biber (Eds.) *The Chamberlain Case: Nation, Law, Memory*. (p. 82). Australian Scholarly Publishing. https://espace.curtin. edu. au/bitstream/hand le/20.500.11937/47384/133645_1558 5_ Dread_Delusion and Globalisation_ From Azaria to Schapelle. pdf?sequence=2&isAllowed=y

4 Partenza, N. (2012, June 12). Comedian Sorry for Azaria Jokes. *Sydney Morning Herald*.

https://www.smh.com.au/national/comedian-sorry-for-azaria-jokes-20120612-207qy.html

5 Clark, J. (2017, November 10). Paris Jackson didn't realise the truth behind a joke she cracked about Australia. *MamaMia*. https://www.mamamia.com.au/paris-jackson-dingo-joke/

6 *The Dingo Ate the Baby Board Game*. Popcultcha.com.
https://www.popcultcha.com.au/the-dingo-ate-the-baby-board-game.html

7 Staines, D. (2006). A Legal Trauma, a Public Trauma: Lindy Chamberlain and the Chamberlain Case. *Studies in Law, Politics and Society, 38*, 158.

8 Fraser (1992) p. 124.

9 For research on the concept of 'mediatization' see Schulz, W. (2004). Reconstructing Mediatization as an Analytical Concept. *European Journal of Communication*, 19(1), 87–101. https://doi.org/10.1177/0267323104040696

10 Couldry (2008) p. 11.

11 Howe (2005) p. 2.

12 March, E. & Steele, G. (2020). High Esteem and Hurting Others Online: Trait Sadism Moderates the Relationship Between Self-Esteem and Internet Trolling. *Cyberpsychology, Behavior, and Social Networking, 23*(7), 441–446. http://doi.org/10.1089/cyber.2019.0652

13 Zerotrousers. *Trolling*. (2009, September 21). Urban Dictionary. https://www.urbandictionary.com/define.php?term=Trolling

14 Donath (1999) p. 45.

15 Donath (1999).

16 For examples see McCosker, A. (2014). Trolling as provocation: YouTube's agonistic publics. *Convergence, 20*(2), 201–217. https://doi.org/10.1177/1354856513501413

17 Rick Astley [@RickAstley]. (2017, July 28). View: https://twitter.com/rickastley/status/890617797956456448?ref_src=twsrc%5Etfw%7Ctwcamp%5Etweetembed%7Ctwterm%5E890617797956456448%7Ctwgr%5E&ref_url=https%3A%2F%2Fwww.abc.net.au%2Fnews%2F2017-0728%2Ftechnology-behind- internet-memes-turns-30%2F8751790

18 Cunningham (1997).

19 Valentine (2017) p. 38; Howe (2005).

20 Howe (2005) p. 14.

21 Valentine (2017) pp. 38–42.

22 Valentine (2017) p. 39.

23 Valentine (2017) p. 42.

24 Howe (2005) p. 300.

25 A smaller committee had been established to 'Free Lindy' in November 1982, the week after her conviction was recorded. Meeting at the Seventh-day Adventist College at Cooranbong, NSW, the group later became known as the 'Chamberlain Innocence Committee', see *Advertiser*, 5 November 1982.

26 *Azaria Newsletter*, 1 April 1984, 2.

27 *Azaria Newsletter*, 7 April 1985.

28 Just five days after the trial verdict, the *Daily Telegraph* interviewed sculptor and Chamberlain advocate Guy Boyd, who said his 'phone had been ringing nonstop since Monday morning and five people were working round-the-clock posting out petitions for people to sign' demanding Lindy's release, see *Daily Telegraph*, 4 November 1982).

29 Ward, P. (1984) *Azaria! What the jury were not told*. PCW.

30 Cyclops. (2012, June 10). *Sensational Azaria Chamberlain case election allegations*. Little Darwin Blogspot. http://littledarwin. blogspot. com/2012/06/sensational-azaria-chamberlain-case.html

31 Howe (2005) p. 28.

32 Flanigan (1984); Rollo (1984).

33 Flanigan (1984)

34 Rollo (1984) pp. 7–8.

35 Flanigan (1984) pp. 12–13.

36 Wilson (1990) p. 16.

37 Munro (1996) p. 15.

38 Chamberlain (1990) p. 561.

39 Young (1989) pp. 12–13.

40 Azaria Newsletter, 9 [August] 1985.

41 Letter from Michael to Lindy Chamberlain (24 March 1984) *Chamberlain Manuscript Collection*. National Library of Australia [Box 69, H–L].

42 Gardiner, S. (2012, June 13) Pressure point: the other one to say sorry to Lindy. *Sydney Morning Herald*.

https://www.smh.com.au/national/pressure-point-the-other-one-to-say-sorry-to-lindy-20120613-209j5.html

43 Turner, G. (2005) *Ending the affair: the decline of television current affairs in Australia*. University of New South Wales, p. 2.

44 Network Ten. (1984). *Azaria: A Question of Evidence*. [Courtesy of the National Film and Sound Archive.]

45 Flanigan (1984).

46 Flanigan (1984).

47 Rosendahl (1984)

48 Howe (2005) p. 61.

49 Azaria Newsletter, 2 June 1984. Copies of the program could be purchased from the Chamberlain Information Service for $35 and $5 on loan.

50 Nugent, M. (2014) *Video Cassette Revolution: The VCR in Australia* [unpublished MA Thesis] Macquarie University p. 5.

51 O'Keeffe (c. 1984)

52 Flanigan (1984) pp. 18–19.

53 Flanigan (1984) p. 1.

54 Flanigan (1984) p. 1.

55 Flanigan (1984) pp. 12–13.

56 *Azaria Newsletter*, 9 [August] 1985.

57 *Daily Telegraph*, 10 November 1982.

58 Cited in *Azaria Newsletter*, 4 [September 18] 1984.

59 *National Times*, 23–29 March 1984.

60 *The Age*, 10 September 1983.

61 Bryson, J. (n.d.) *Biography*. http://www.johnbryson.net/

62 Howe (2005) p. 28.

63 Howe (2005) p. 18.

64 Young (1989) p. 14.

65 Bryson (2000) p. 394.

66 Watts, M. (October 2013) Interview with John Bryson, *Griffith Review*

https://www.griffithreview.com/articles/interview-with-john-bryson/

67 Howe (2005) p. 12.

68 Howe (2005) p. 223.

69 Howe (2005) p. 2.

70 Howe (2005) p. 300.

71 Lumby (1999) pp. 84–5.

Chapter 3: Celebrity Before Instagram

1 *The Age*, 16 September 1988.

2 Marwick, A.E. (2015). Instafame: Luxury Selfies in the Attention Economy. *Public Culture*, 27(1), 137–160.

3 Lumby (1999) p. 216.

4 According to renowned celebrity studies academic P David Marshall, personas are 'public displays of the self' that constitute 'a strategic form of public identity', see Marshall, P.D. (2016). *The celebrity persona pandemic*. University of Minnesota Press p. 16.

5 See the 'Timeline of Events' on Lindy Chamberlain's personal website https://lindychamberlain.com/the-story/timeline-of-events/

6 Marshall, P.D. (1997). *Celebrity and Power: Fame in Contemporary Culture*. University of Minnesota Press p. 5.

7 Boorstin, D. (1961). *The Image: A Guide to Pseudo-events in America*. Harper and Row p. 58.

8 Marshall (1997) pp. 5–9.

9 Marshall (1997) p. 6.

10 Marshall (1997) p. 6.

11 Senft, T.M. (2008). *Camgirls: celebrity and community in the age of social networks*. Peter Lang p. 25.

12 Rojek, C. (2001). *Celebrity*. Reaktion pp. 17–22.

13 Turner, G., Bonner, B., & Marshall, P.D. (2000). *Fame Games: The Production of Celebrity in Australia*. Cambridge University Press.

14 Elsewhere I have argued that criminally implicated female celebrities such as Lindy Chamberlain and convicted Bali drug trafficker Schapelle Corby are better classed as 'deviant divas' because their desirability was bound up with their transgressions and they became screens on whom anxieties about the performance of gender were projected. See Middleweek, B. (2017). Deviant divas: Lindy Chamberlain and Schapelle Corby and the case for a new category of celebrity for criminally implicated women. *Crime, Media, Culture*, 13(1), 85–105. DOI: 10.1177/1741659016646596.

15 Rojek (2001).

16 Turner, Bonner & Marshall (2000) p. 48.

17 Turner, Bonner & Marshall (2000) p. 2, p. 45.

18 Turner, Bonner & Marshall (2000).

19 Marshall (1997) pp. 207–8.

20 Turner, Bonner & Marshall (2000) p. 34.

21 Gleeson, D.J. (2012). George William Sydney Fitzpatrick (1884–1948): An Australian Public Relations 'pioneer.' *Asia Pacific Public Relations Journal, 13*(2), 2-12.

22 Tynan, L. (2011). Public Relations: Spin Cycle. In J. Bainbridge, N. Goc & L. Tynan (Eds.), *Media and Journalism: New Approaches to Theory and Practice* (2nd ed, p. 141). Oxford University Press.

23 Marshall (1997) p. 210.

24 *The Bulletin*, 26 November 1985.

25 Little, J. (1994). *Inside 60 Minutes: The story behind the stories*. Allen & Unwin p. 150.

26 Little (1994) p. 152.

27 Malden, A.N. (1987, June 15). Witch-Hunt: Lindy and the Australian Psyche. *Time Australia* p. 24.

28 *The Bulletin*, 26 November 1985.

29 Little (1994) 151.

30 Nine Network. (1986, March 2). *60 Minutes.*

31 Nine Network. (1986, March 2). *60 Minutes.*

32 Howe (2005) p. 54.

33 Lumby (1999) pp. 41–3.

34 Lumby (1999) pp. 41–3.

35 Turner, Bonner & Marshall (2000).

36 Turner, Bonner & Marshall (2000) p. 11.

37 Lumby (1999) pp. 41–3.

38 Derryn Hinch's eponymous current affairs program was broadcast on Channel Seven from 1987 to 1991, and on the Ten Network from 1992 to 1994.

39 Hemphill, B. (2012, August 28). Derryn Hinch – the story behind the human headline. *Mumbrella.*

https://mumbrella.com.au/derryn-hinch-the-story-behind-the-human-headline-112322

40 Turner, G. (2005). p. 1, p. 52.

41 *Australian Women's Weekly*, March 1986.

42 *Australian Women's Weekly*, March 1986.

43 *Australian Women's Weekly*, March 1986.

44 Howe (2005) pp. 255–6.

45 Howe (2005) p. 256.

46 Lumby, C. (1999). Media Culpa: Tabloid Media, Democracy and the Public Sphere. *The Sydney Papers, 11*(3, Winter), 113.

47 *Australian Women's Weekly*, March 1986.

48 Howe (2005) p. 8.

49 *Australian Women's Weekly*, March 1986.

50 Turner, Bonner & Marshall (2000) p. 122.

51 Hermes, J. (1995). *Reading Women's Magazines: An Analysis of Everyday Media Use*. Polity Press p. 36.

52 Turner, G. (2004). *Understanding Celebrity*. Sage Publications p. 85.

53 Turner (2004) pp. 38–41.

54 *The Age*, 2 February 1982.

55 *Daily Telegraph*, 4 November 1982.

56 Carlisle, W. Background Briefing (2005, July 24). *ABC Radio National*.

57 Shears (1982) p. 152.

58 Simmonds, J. (1982). *Azaria: Wednesday's Child*. TPNL Books p. 127.

59 *Sun-Herald*, 19 September 1982.

60 *Sydney Morning Herald*, 30 October 1982.

61 *Daily Telegraph*, 1 November 1982.

62 Crispin, K. (1987). *The Crown versus Chamberlain: 1980–1987*. Albatross Books p. 115.

63 Crispin (1987) p. 115.

64 *Sun-Herald*, 26 September 1982.

65 Lumby (1999) p. 25.

66 Quoted in *Australian Women's Weekly*, March 1986.

67 Simmonds (1982) p. 48.

68 Simmonds (1982) p. 48.

69 Shears (1982) p. 185.

70 Howe (2005) p. 227.

71 *The Herald*, 2 February 1982.

72 Howe (2005) p. 228; see also Wilson, P. (1987). *Media Distortions of Crime and Miscarriages of Justice*. Australian Institute of Criminology p. 152.

73 *The Bulletin*, 26 November 1985.

74 *Australian Women's Weekly*, March 1986.

75 *Sunday Territorian*, 27 October 1985.

76 Baird, J. (2004). *Media Tarts: How the Australian press frames female politicians*. Scribe Publications p. 5.

77 Warner, M. (1993). The Mass Public and the Mass Subject. In B. Robbins (Ed.). *The Phantom Public Sphere* (p. 250). University of Minnesota Press.

78 Greer, G. (1970). *The Female Eunuch*. Hart-Davis, MacGibbon, Limited p. 279.

79 Eisenstein, H. (1996). *Inside Agitators: Australian Femocrats and the State*. Allen and Unwin.

80 Sawer, M. (2007). Australia: The Fall of the Femocrat. In J. Outshoorn & J. Kantola J (Eds.), *Changing State Feminism* (pp. 20-40). Palgrave Macmillan. https://doi.org/10.1057/9780230591424_2

81 For a detailed timeline of achievements by and for Australian women from 1788 to 2001, see Summers, A. (2001). *Damned Whores and God's Police* (2nd rev. ed). Penguin pp. 547–63.

82 Johnson, D. (1984). From Fairy to Witch: Imagery and Myth in the Azaria Case. In Howe (2005) p. 147.

83 Shears (1982) p. 149.

84 Middleweek (2017).

85 Lumby (1999) p. 2, pp. 4–5.

86 Howe (2005) p. 131, p. 227 and p. 157.

87 *New Idea*, 27 November 2004.

Chapter 4: Sorry, Not Sorry

1 *Advertiser*, 16 September 1988.

2 Extract from the election policy speech of the Leader of the Opposition, Bob Hawke, who won a landslide victory against Prime Minister Malcolm Fraser in the election held 5 March 1983, cited in Kelly, P. (2008). *The end of certainty: Power, politics and business in Australia*. Allen and Unwin p. 19.

3 Cruickshank, J. (2016, May 26). Sorry (Not Sorry): Australia's History of Ambivalence to Aboriginal Activism. *ABC Religion and Ethics.*

https://www.abc.net.au/religion/sorry-not-sorry-australias-history-of-ambivalence-to-aboriginal-/10096954

4 Short, D. (2012). When sorry isn't good enough: Official remembrance and reconciliation in Australia. *Memory Studies*, 5(3), 293–304.

5 Barta, T. (2008). Sorry, and not sorry, in Australia: How the apology to the stolen generations buried a history of genocide. *Journal of Genocide Research, 10*(2), 201–14.

6 Hunter, R. (1993). Before Cook and After Cook: Land Rights and Legal Histories in Australia. *Social & Legal Studies, 2*(4), 494. https://doi.org/10.1177/096466399300200407

7 Seal, G. (1987). Azaria Chamberlain and the Media Charivari. *Australian Folklore, 1*(March), 76.

8 Norman, H. (2015). *What do we want? A political history of Aboriginal land rights in New South Wales*. Aboriginal Studies Press p. xii.

9 Hunter (1993) p. 492.

10 Langton, M. (c. 1988). Labor and Land Rights: The Great Surrender. *Australian Left Review*, 33–37.

https://ro.uow.edu.au/cgi/viewcontent.cgi?article=2326&context=alr

11 *Sydney Morning Herald*, 26 October 1985.

12 *Sydney Morning Herald*, 26 October 1985.

13 *Courier-Mail*, 28 October 1985.

14 *Sydney Morning Herald*, 26 October 1985.

15 *Advertiser*, 26 October 1985.

16 *Sydney Morning Herald*, 21 May 1985.

17 *Sydney Morning Herald*, 18 December 1985.

18 *Sydney Morning Herald*, 18 December 1985.

19 Schaffer, K. (1988). *Women and the Bush: Forces of Desire in the Australian Cultural Tradition*. Cambridge University Press p. 52.

20 Schaffer (1988) p. 4.

21 Carter, D. (1996). Crocs in frocks: Landscape and nation in the 1990s. *Journal of Australian Studies, 20*(49), 90. DOI: 10.1080/14443059609391746

22 Rooney, B, (2007). Desert Hauntings, Public Interiors and National Modernity: From The Overlanders to Walkabout and Japanese Story. *Southerly*, 67(1–2), 416.

23 *Sydney Morning Herald*, 21 May 1985.

24 *Advertiser*, 26 October 1985.

25 *Sydney Morning Herald*, 5 November 1985.

26 *Sydney Morning Herald*, 5 November 1985.

27 Kuntsman, A. (2017). Introduction: Whose selfie citizenship? In A. Kuntsman (Ed.), *Selfie Citizenship* (pp. 13-20). Manchester: Palgrave Macmillan.

28 *Courier-Mail*, 28 October 1985.

29 *Courier-Mail*, 26 October 1985.

30 *Advertiser*, 2–7 February 1986.

31 *Advertiser*, 7 February 1986.

32 *Advertiser*, 7 February 1986.

33 *Advertiser*, 2–7 February 1986; *Daily Telegraph*, 7 February 1986 and *Courier-Mail*, 2–7 February 1986.

34 *Sunday Territorian*, 27 October 1985.

35 *Sunday Territorian*, 27 October 1985.

36 Northern Territory Parks and Wildlife Commission. (December 1978). *Development Plan*.

37 *Sydney Morning Herald*, 12 November 1983.

38 *Sydney Morning Herald*, 19 April 1986.

39 *Sydney Morning Herald*, 19 April 1986.

40 *Sydney Morning Herald*, 19 April 1986.

41 *Sunday Press*, 21 August 1983.

42 *Sunday Press*, 21 August 1983.

43 Clark in Stokes, G. (1997). *The Politics of Identity in Australia.* Cambridge University Press p. 2.

44 Hawley, J., Hewett, T. & Monaghan, D. (2018, 26 January). 30 years on: Pomp and protest as Sydney celebrates the Bicentenary. *Sydney Morning Herald.*

45 Hawley, Hewett & Monaghan (2018).

46 Meadows, M. & Oldham, C. (1991). Racism and the Dominant Ideology Aborigines, Television News and the Bicentenary. *Media Information Australia*, *60*(1), 30. https://doi.org/10.1177/1329878X9106000108

47 *Sydney Morning Herald*, 18 June 1988.

48 *Sydney Morning Herald*, 18 June 1988.

49 *Sydney Morning Herald*, 18 June 1988.

50 *Sydney Morning Herald*, 18 June 1988.

51 Adams, P. (2018, September 8). Australia Live simulcast. *The Weekend Australian.*

https://www.theaustralian.com.au/weekend-australian-magazine/australia-live-simulcast-1988/news-story/4a129da78d08fa75343ba5b2397809eb

52 Carter, D. (1998). The Wide Brown Land on the Small Grey Screen: The Nature of Landscape on Australian Television. *Journal of Australian Studies*, (September), 2.

53 *The Herald*, 15 September 1988.

54 *Daily Telegraph*, 16 September 1988.

55 *Daily Mirror*, 16 September 1988.

56 *Daily Telegraph*, 16 September 1988.

57 Malden, A.N. (1987). Witch-Hunt: Lindy and the Australian Psyche. *Time Australia*, (15 June), p. 24, p. 33.

58 *Courier-Mail*, 16 September 1988.

59 *Daily Mail*, 16 September 1988.

60 Quoted in *Daily Mail*, 16 September 1988.

61 *Advertiser*, 26 October 1985.

62 *Sun-Herald*, 7 August 1988.

63 Staines, D. (2006). A Legal Trauma, A Public Trauma: Lindy Chamberlain and the Chamberlain Case. *Studies in Law, Politics and Society, 38*, 168.

64 Staines (2006) p. 155.

65 Sanders, N. (1993). Azaria Chamberlain and popular culture. In J. Frow & M. Morris. (Eds.), *Australian Cultural Studies: A Reader* (p. 94). Allen & Unwin.

66 Higgins, C. (1994). Naturalising Horror Stories: Australian Crime News as Popular Culture. In I. Craven (Ed.), *Australian Popular Culture* (pp. 139-40). Cambridge University Press.

67 *Sydney Morning Herald*, 15 March 1988.

68 For example, see articles by Johnson (1984), Catherine Rogers (1986) and Julie Marcus (1989) in Howe (2005); and Sanders (1982) in Frow and Morris (1993).

69 *Advertiser*, 16 September 1988.

70 White, R. (1981). *Inventing Australia: Images and Identity 1699–1980*. Allen and Unwin p. 169.

71 Turner, G. (Ed.) (1993). *Nation, Culture, Text: Australian Cultural and Media Studies*. Routledge.

72 Murray, S. (Ed.) (1994). *Australian Cinema*. Allen and Unwin pp. 95–6.

73 Malden, A.N. (1987). Witch-Hunt: Lindy and the Australian Psyche. *Time Australia*, (15 June), 24.

74 *New York Times*, 11 November 1988.

75 White (1981) p. 170.

76 Note that the figure quoted does not identify either $US or $AUD currency, see Beard, V. (2000). Evil Angels. [Review of the film *Evil Angels*, dir. F. Schepisi]. School of Media Communication and Culture, Murdoch University p. 6. http://wwwmcc.murdoch.edu.au/ReadingRoom/film/dbase/2000/EvilAngels.html

77 Bennett, T. (1992). *Celebrating the Nation: A Critical Study of Australia's Bicentenary*. Allen and Unwin p. 184.

78 Pearce, S.M. (1993). *Museums, Objects and Collections: A Cultural Study*. Smithsonian Institution Press p. 26.

79 Pearce (1993) p. 24.

80 Kenneally in Malden (1987) p. 24.

Conclusion

1 Middleweek, B. & McKay, B. (2012, March 26). Interview with journalist Bill Hitchings who was reporting the Chamberlain story for the Melbourne tabloids *The Herald* and T*he Sun-News Pictorial.*

2 Howe (2005) p. 223; see also Goldsworthy (1986) and Rogers (1986) in Howe (2005).

3 Howe (2005) p. 247.

4 Howe (2005) pp. 249–50.

5 Howe (2005) p. 223.

6 Howe (2005) p. 226.

7 Marcus (1989) in Howe (2005) p. 202.

8 Howe (2005) p. 119.

9 Howe (2005) p. 120.

10 Howe (2005) p. 2.

11 Dawson, N. (2002). Lindy Chamberlain: a personal visual response, Doctor of Creative Arts thesis, University of Wollongong. Available at: https://ro.uow.edu.au/cgi/viewcontent.cgi?article=1921&context=theses (Accessed 21 January 2021)

12 Howe (2005) p. 12, p. 10.

13 Howe (2005) p. 14.

14 Schwartz, D. (2012, June 17). Lessons Learned from Azaria Chamberlain. *ABC Correspondents Report.* https://www.abc.net.au/correspondents/content/2012/s3526694. html

15 Enker, D. (2020, September 20). Forty years on, Lindy Chamberlain's tragedy continues to reverberate. *Sydney Morning Herald.* https://www.smh.com.au/culture/tv-and-radio/forty-years-on-lindy-chamberlain-s-tragedy-continues-to-reverberate-

20200916-p55wcv.html

16 Middleweek, B. & McKay, B. (2012, March 26). Interview with Bill Hitchings via phone.

17 Middleweek, B. & McKay, B. (2012, March 26). Interview with Bill Hitchings via phone.

18 Moorhouse, F. (1993). The Azaria Chamberlain Case (1980–86): Hysteria and the Intellectuals. *Australian Cultural History, 12*, 169.

19 Deuze, M. (2011). Media life. *Media, Culture & Society*, 33(1), 137–48. https://doi.org/10.1177/0163443710386518

20 McQuail, D. (2010). *McQuail's Mass Communication Theory: An Introduction* (6th ed.). Sage Publications p. 312.

21 Lumby (1999) pp. 23–4.

22 Cunningham, A. (1997). Icons, Symbolism and Recordkeeping: The Lindy Chamberlain and Eddie Mabo Papers in the National Library of Australia. *Australian Academic and Research Libraries, 28*(2), 103.

23 *New Idea*, 29 June 2002.

24 *New Idea*, 11 June 2005.

25 See Goldsworthy (1986) and Marcus (1989) in Howe (2005).

26 Malden (1987).

INDEX

www.ingramcontent.com/pod-product-compliance
Ingram Content Group Australia Pty Ltd
76 Discovery Rd, Dandenong South VIC 3175, AU
AUHW020136130726
429791AU00003B/106

9 781922 454454